CLAUDEL: A REAPPRAISAL

CLAUDEL:

a reappraisal

edited by

RICHARD GRIFFITHS

Dufour Editions, Chester Springs, Pa.

Nihil obstat F. J. BARTLETT
           Censor

Imprimatur ✠ PATRICK CASEY VG

Westminster, 9.ix.68

    The Nihil obstat *and* Imprimatur *are a declaration that a book or pamphlet is considered to be free from doctrinal or moral error. It is not implied that those who have granted the* Nihil obstat *and* Imprimatur *agree with the contents, opinions or statements expressed.*

LIBRARY OF CONGRESS CATALOG CARD NUMBER: 73-88601

© 1968 RAPP AND WHITING LIMITED
76 NEW OXFORD STREET LONDON WCI
FIRST PUBLISHED IN THE UNITED STATES
OF AMERICA 1970 BY DUFOUR EDITIONS INC
CHESTER SPRINGS PA
PRINTED IN GREAT BRITAIN

Contents

v

Preface

THE IDEA for this volume first came to light at a lunch-party given in London by Mrs Marie-Sygne James, to which Madame Renée Nantet, of the *Comité du Centenaire de la Naissance de Paul Claudel*, had come in order to discuss with British Claudelians the possible forms of action which might be taken here for the celebration of the 1968 centenary.

The thing which became immediately obvious was the amount of work which was in progress on Claudel in this, a country traditionally believed to be lacking in interest in this author. It was decided to set on foot a volume consisting of articles written by people resident in the British Isles, together with one or two contributions on subjects connected with Britain, which could be written by people from outside this country. In this way a truly British volume could be produced for the centenary.

It was only after I had formed my team of writers that I realized how few of them were in fact English: in origin, one was Polish, one Roumanian, one Austrian, one Swiss, two French; then came the Celtic fringe, with three Welsh (one of them partly of Irish extraction), and one Irish; and finally, there were three Englishmen left. All but one of the contributors are, however, resident in the British Isles; and they give what I would consider a typical example of the variety and worth of our university and cultural life, while nevertheless bearing out the view I already held, that it is on the whole the Celts, of all the nations in the British Isles, who find themselves most attracted to the writings of Claudel.

My thanks are above all due to Madame Nantet, for the idea behind the volume, and to the contributors for the hard work they have put into it; to all those who have placed documents at the disposal of the contributors, and particularly to Dr Egon Wellesz, Mrs O. Sowerby, and the *Société Paul Claudel*; to Miss Annette Kahn for her skilful translation of the articles by Gilbert Gadoffre and Alexander Mavrocordato; and to our publishers, Messrs. Rapp and Whiting, for their courteous and generous help.

RICHARD GRIFFITHS

Abbreviations: Pl. = Bibliothèque de la Pléiade. *NRF* = Nouvelle Revue Française. *RHLF* = Revue d'Histoire litteraire de la France.

List of contributors

ANNIE BARNES. University Reader in French, St Anne's College, Oxford.

ERNEST BEAUMONT. Author of *The Theme of Beatrice in the Plays of Claudel* (1954), and of numerous other publications upon French Literature. Reader in French at the University of Southampton.

ELFRIEDA DUBOIS. Author of *Portrait of Léon Bloy* (1950). Senior lecturer in French, University of Newcastle.

GILBERT GADOFFRE. Author, among other things, of works upon Ronsard and Descartes. Head of the *Institut Collegial Européen*. Professor of Modern French Literature in the University of Manchester.

RICHARD GRIFFITHS. Author of *The Reactionary Revolution* (1966). Fellow of Brasenose College, Oxford.

BERNARD HOWELLS. Lecturer at King's College, University of London.

MOYA LAVERTY. Lecturer at the Queen's University, Belfast.

WITOLD LEITGEBER. Formerly foreign correspondent of *Kurier Poznański* in Paris. Member of staff of BBC European services since 1949.

PRINCE ALEXANDER MAVROCORDATO. Author of *L'Ode de Paul Claudel* (1955), and *Anglo-American Influences in Paul Claudel* (1) *Coventry Patmore* (1964). Head of the English department, University of Nantes.

JEAN MOUTON. Author of *Le Style de Marcel Proust* (1948), *Charles du Bos* (1954), and other works. Director of Studies at the Institut Français, London.

PATRICK MCCARTHY. Fellow of Selwyn College, Cambridge.

EDWARD LUCIE-SMITH. Translator, among other things, of *Cinq grandes odes*. Writer and free-lance journalist.

MICHAEL WOOD. Formerly Fellow of St John's College, Cambridge. Now a free-lance writer and journalist.

1 · Introduction: Claudel in all honesty

RICHARD GRIFFITHS

EITHER ONE IS FOR Paul Claudel, or else one is wholeheartedly against him. What is significant, but not wholly surprising, is the large number of people, both in England and France, who come under the second category. And while this is particularly galling to those of us who believe him to be the best serious playwright in the French language since the seventeenth century, we are nevertheless forced to admit that the fault lies largely on our side. An over-exclusive view of this poet, concentrating to a large degree on characteristics of his work which are incidental rather than central to his greatness, and which flatter our own hobby-horses rather than his aesthetic intentions, has been the main contribution of the literary critics to the maintenance of his fame. Small wonder that those who do not share these hobby-horses should shy off from an author whose whole work, if his admirers are to be trusted, rests on these things.

An understanding of the workings of Claudel's particular form of Catholicism, of its orthodox and its unorthodox features, is for example, extremely useful, indeed essential, to a full comprehension of the stresses which lie behind the action of his plays. His religious beliefs, as we shall see, are among the things which are instrumental in making his theatre so much more effective than that of the other Symbolist playwrights. But to go on from this, as so many have done, to make his religious beliefs the central reason for his success, and to make our appreciation of his works rest on a religious fellow-feeling with the author, is to destroy him as an author with any real claim to serious consideration. Explicitly or implicitly, much Claudel criticism has taken the familiar line which equates the terms 'Catholicism' and 'literary excellence'. Even the style in which it is written often gives it away.

Such an attitude can only lower Claudel. For if being a Catholic is a cause for literary fame, what of Émile Baumann? What of

Adolphe Retté? What of so many other writers whose memory could not be safeguarded even by the cohorts of Catholic criticism? Claudel's religion, as a basis for conflict in his plays (and it is at its best for this purpose when it is at its most unorthodox, or its most muddled) serves an excellent purpose. This is a literary purpose, however. Once it is viewed as such, once Claudel is viewed first and foremost as a playwright, then many of the adverse preconceptions which have been formed in the mind of the general public will be dispersed. Claudel must be seen as a playwright who is a Catholic, rather than a Catholic who is a playwright. This is a fact which the writers in the present volume have seen quite clearly.

Once the veils of hagiography have been drawn away, what do we see? Before anything else, the man who made a success of the Symbolist theatre. It is a fascinating exercise to place any play by Claudel alongside a play by Maeterlinck, or Villiers de l'Isle Adam's *Axël*. There is no comparison at all. And while it would be tempting to lay this entirely at the door of Claudel's dramatic genius (which, heaven knows, he possessed in abundance), and to leave the matter there, it is perhaps more constructive to look at some of the reasons for Claudel's success and the comparative failure of the others.

The Symbolist theatre had, in its beginnings, much the same form of difficulty as the Symbolist novel. Techniques which were admirably suited to the shorter form of lyric poetry were here being transferred into far more large-scale works, with a resultant slackness and looseness of construction, and a certain incoherence of intention. The Symbolist novel never really got beyond the starting-post; the Symbolist theatre, however, partly through the varying media in which it could work (the frequence and length of the stage-directions in *Axël* are significant here), and partly through certain attributes which it took over from the Romantic theatre, had a certain modicum of success. Despite this, it still suffered from those drawbacks to which we have referred. Atmosphere it succeeded in creating by various means of suggestion, and nobody could be dissatisfied by the feeling of vagueness which fills, for example, *Pelléas et Mélisande*. But drama demands more than this. Vagueness and the suggestion of reality, of the reality of essence, are the mainstay of Symbolist poetry; but a theatre audience, much as it may enjoy wallowing in 'atmosphere', eventually demands more: a centre around which the poet's symbols may form themselves, a coherent direction to the plot, however allusive it may be, and above all the sense of struggle and tension, whether personal or ideological.

Such was the scene when Claudel produced his first play, *Tête d'or*, in 1889. This vast Wagnerian fresco, though it is far nearer to the rest of the Symbolist theatre than his later plays, nevertheless still strikes us with its power and wild beauty. These are two of the attributes which stamp Claudel as a great playwright, to such an extent that even those who feel themselves obliged to disapprove of his ideas, and to feel that an opinion of his ideas is the most important way to approach him critically, are occasionally forced to exclaim 'Claudel, hélas', when asked who is the greatest French playwright of the nineteenth and twentieth centuries; power of expression, and beauty of verse. The Claudelian *verset* can already be heard in this play, with its rhythmic energy, vocal beauty and emotional intensity fully formed; those who saw the recent revival of this play in Paris, with Alain Cuny in the main part, will realize the extent to which these characteristics of the verse dominate the play.

No collection of studies of Claudel would be complete without at least one article on his verse; and we are happy to have a study in this volume of some of the Biblical influences upon its form, by Dr Elfrieda Dubois.

Power and beauty of verse alone, however, do not create a play, much as they may do to enhance it. *Tête d'or*, exciting as it is as an early example of Claudel's work, giving glimpses of the genius that is to come, would not stand on its own, would no more have survived for modern audiences than *Axël*, *Monna Vanna* or (had it not been for Debussy) *Pelléas et Mélisande*. It was in Claudel's subsequent plays that two further characteristics came to the fore, which transformed the Symbolist theatre into something more coherent and vital. These characteristics were (i) A central core, around which the poet's symbols could group themselves; a core, moreover, which provided symbols which to a great extent already had a certain amount of meaning for the spectator, but on which could be built up far more in the way of allusion, because of the firm base from which it started. (ii) In the later plays, the effects of lived experience, which could make of the poet's characters not just walking symbols, but three-dimensional beings of flesh and blood, whose interactions can be seen both on the human and the symbolic plane.

The central core around which his ideas were eventually to revolve was, of course, Catholicism. Claudel was converted in 1886, and received into the Church in 1890. In some of his earlier plays, and particularly in the first version of *La Ville* (1890), other systems of thought, and their attendant battery of symbols (such as anarchism's images of fire and destruction) mingle with the Christian themes. But the richest source of imagery remains the Catholic faith. Not only does it have a wider and more universal range of symbols than the other systems that have been mentioned; this range of symbols is also more universally accessible to the audience in a country which is Catholic in formation if not in faith. For every person, according to their faith or lack of it, the symbols used may have a different meaning, may raise more or less meaningful overtones. But they will mean *something*, will suggest *something*, and that something will have a coherence and a shape that was lacking in Symbolist drama up to this time.

Not only does Claudel's Catholicism provide him with a basis for his Symbolism; it also, because of the special form which his belief takes, gives him opportunities for struggle and tension in his plays which might have been lacking if his belief had been more orthodox. His views on suffering and expiation, his conception of human and sexual relationships, of the 'order' of marriage and the necessity for lovers' separation, all lead to tension of a particularly dramatic kind; just as his view of the divine equilibrium, of mystical substitution, and of the ineluctable pattern of history give a kind of fatality to these struggles by which man's liberty to act is placed within a wider context, that of the liberty to obey.

That all this is dramatic cannot be denied. And the fact of not being a Catholic in no way prevents one from appreciating it. In fact, belief is in no way essential. How many Catholics of our own day would subscribe to all Claudel's beliefs? As with much great theatre, I believe that the audience must suspend judgment, and accept for the duration of the play that its suppositions are true. Is this not what we do with Greek tragedy? And is this not what an atheist must do in (for example) *Polyeucte, Saint Genest* or even *Phèdre*? Claudel's drama depends upon one particular type of metaphysical system; but then, so does (explicitly or implicitly) all drama.

Claudel's beliefs, as I have said, are often unorthodox. Some of this stems from the particular forms which Catholicism took in the France of his era; some of it comes from his reading, and his methods of reading; but even more seems to come from his own emotional problems, as they came into contact with his religious fervour. This unorthodoxy, and the problems it raises, contribute much to the effect of Claudel's plays, and therefore warrant extensive study. For this reason one is particularly glad to have, in this volume, Ernest Beaumont's study of Claudel's view of the figure of Wisdom, or Sophia, and Bernard Howells's article on the problems raised by the play *Partage de midi*, while Michael Wood's pages on *Le Soulier de satin* take us on to completely new ground with the exposition of Claudel's view of God's creation being a play like Claudel's own (with all the various planes of meaning that that entails).

Catholicism of a particular kind is, then, the central core around which Claudel's Symbolism forms itself, and also a means to dramatic conflict and tension. This latter is added to, in the later plays, by a sense of immediacy and of personal involvement which is new to the Symbolist theatre, and which represents Claudel's other great contribution to the form.

The Symbolist theatre had not, on the whole, been renowned for its immediacy and human interest. Dealing as it did above all with concepts which were to be expressed in symbolic form, it tended to make of its characters two-dimensional entities whose main function was to stand for certain attitudes or ideas. Any conflict that there was tended to be explicable only in terms of these higher systems of thought, with human relationships becoming merely representative of such things as the marriage of concepts, etc.; or else, if real human relationships were involved, they tended to be expressed in the most abstract and vague of terms, as in *Pelléas*, so that one was often unsure as to the extent of what was being suggested.

For about the first half of Claudel's career his plays, though far superior to those of the other Symbolists for the reasons we have already discussed, nevertheless retained this aspect of pure Symbolism. We can, it is true, see hints beneath the surface of the emotional stresses which the poet was undergoing; hints, however, which are far clearer to us, with our hindsight based on our knowledge of his later plays, than they would have been to a contemporary audience which did not have the literary critic's urge to psychoanalysis. The main impression is still, as with the other playwrights of the era, one of two-dimensional characters who are there in order to symbolize various important facts and attitudes. Nowhere is this more true than in the second version of *La Ville* (1897), where Lâla's movements from man to man are prompted not by humanly explicable emotions, but by symbolic necessity. This is in no way to condemn these plays of Claudel's. As they stand, they are already evidence of a playwright far greater than France had seen for many years, and who, even if he had not written his later plays, would still have been in the forefront of the French literature of his period. It is his later plays, however, those written from 1900 onwards, on which his greatest fame rests, and justifiably so.

What happened at this period to change the direction of his work so greatly? Two things of importance. The first, on the level of Claudel's religious thinking, was the acceptance of various ideas upon vicarious suffering, which were to form the basis for much of the conflict in his later plays, explaining as they did the problems of sin and redemption, suffering and expiation, as parts of a divine plan, a divine equilibrium for the world. With the acceptance of these ideas, and the new interpretations which Claudel himself put upon them, the religious core which has been described as of such importance to Claudel as a dramatic author achieved its greatest effects, in such plays as *L'Annonce faite à Marie* (1910), (a completely revised version of the *La Jeune Fille Violaine* of 1892 and 1898, and therefore an excellent example for study of the impact of these new religious ideas), *L'Otage* (1909), *Le Pain dur* (1914), *Le Père humilié* (1916) and, of course, *Le Soulier de satin* (1924).

The second thing, which is perhaps even more important in its effect on Claudel as a dramatist, was the great emotional crisis he underwent in the early years of the century. Having been refused his desire to become a monk in the Benedictine order, at Ligugé in 1900, Claudel went through spiritual anguish, in the belief that God had in some way refused him, cast him adrift, and condemned him to wander aimlessly in his old life. It was while he was in this state, and during the course of a voyage by ship to China to take up a new diplomatic post, that he began the passionate love affair with a married woman which was to be the basis for his play *Partage de midi* (1905), and which was to colour the rest of his dramatic output. The complications and difficulties caused by this affair, and his subsequent sense of guilt, together with the need to incorporate his feelings and experience within a Christian philosophy, are discussed by Bernard Howells in his article in this volume. In the play *Partage de midi*, as both Bernard Howells and Ernest Beaumont point out, the conflict between emotional necessity and theological design is not fully worked out; indeed, from this aspect the play is something of a muddle. In later plays, this conflict eventually produces many of the stranger aspects of Claudel's theological outlook, and, while many of the problems are thus resolved, others occasionally have to be by-passed by various means, stylistic and otherwise.

Still, we must come back to this. What is important in this new influence on Claudel is that from now onwards his characters are

7

three-dimensional people dealing with human problems, even though these problems by the nature of things have other planes, symbolic and metaphysical, on which they must be worked out. Where the characters of Villiers, of Maeterlinck and even of the early Claudel had, in one sense escaped from the first term of the symbol, i.e. the reality on which the symbolic system is based, Claudel now provided that first term, and the metaphysical system (in his case an unorthodox Catholic one) to which his symbols are intended to point is closely bound up with this reality. The separated lovers in his later plays continue to be Mésa and Ysé, Paul Claudel and his Polish mistress of the years just before *Partage de midi*. The problem of this human love and its true meaning continues to be the central theme. And Claudel's characters live, and experience human anguish. His discussion of religious and philosophical themes is made real to us by this human concern. It is perhaps for this reason that *Partage de midi*, despite the element of muddle in the treatment of the themes involved, is by the very immediacy of its subject, the most popular of Claudel's plays when performed on the stage. The author's very uncertainty about the meaning of the problems involved makes the struggle of the characters even more credible.

Now while, as we have seen, Claudel's religious ideas were an extremely efficacious basis for his drama, and particularly because the odd and unorthodox elements in them led to even more excuse for dramatic struggle and conflict than might otherwise have been the case, these ideas and the issues that evolve from them are often very unclear or even muddled. Some of the reasons for this lies in the basic conflict of ideas which Bernard Howells has so clearly noticed in *Partage de midi*, and which continues, though to a lesser extent, in the later plays. Some if it stems from Claudel's own methods of thought and of reading. For though he juggles with many complicated philosophical and religious issues, Claudel was not in the real sense of the word an intellectual. His over-simplified view of many problems makes this clear; and his habit, when reading the works of others, of picking out only those items which were of use to him, and ignoring the rest, has been noted by several critics. His approach to St Thomas is typical of this, in that, faced by what must to any modern man be an alien system of thought needing commentary, Claudel claimed that he had picked up the language of scholasticism as he went along, found the text amazingly simple, and rejected the texts of the commentators because they were far too complicated. The indigestible way in which Claudel presented certain separate ideas of St Thomas in his play *Le Repos du septième jour* (1896), and the unfortunate way in which he allows the opinions based on these ideas occasionally to contradict each other, shows that, as in other cases, he has used the author only in so far as he fits in with his own preconceptions. 'In Claudel's plays', as I have said elsewhere, 'a certain amount of intellectual paraphernalia adorns what are essentially simple, violent beliefs and passions.' This is, in a sense, what makes him so effective dramatically. And where the simple systems that he has evolved, for example those in relation to love, separation and marriage, seem to be coming to the point where a specific statement is required with regard to the central issues, we can sense the poet, in whose own mind these issues have not been, and cannot be, fully resolved, desperately creating a smokescreen of words to cloud the scene until the crisis is past.

These idiosyncratic but indeed infrequent moments are of little importance, however, except in so far as they show us how little Claudel's success depends upon the coherent exposition of ideas. His greatness depends on things other than this: power, violence and depth of emotion, evocative symbols set in a coherent scheme, the creation of suggestion and atmosphere, the sense of struggle and tension; and, above all, the magnificent, colourful verse in which all this is set. Claudel himself knew that it was this verse form, so revolutionary in the freedom and subtlety of its rhythms, which created one of his greatest claims to fame.

This is, above all, *dramatic* poetry. Just as the dramatists of the French Renaissance had created verse which, by rhetorical necessity, had to be contained in dramatic form (even though in their case drama had been in a sense a series of poems), so Claudel, in a form that is far more dramatic (in a modern sense) than theirs,

produces verse which in any other context would miss its effect.
The rhetorical power of it can, when transferred to lyric verse, be
bathetic. Only occasionally, when the grandeur of the design
matches that of his drama, as in *Cinq grandes odes* (of which this
volume contains a study by Edward Lucie-Smith), does his poetry
achieve the same success. That is, except in those cases where the
poet abandons the manner of his dramatic poetry, and produces
a simple and moving style of a different type, as in the poem 'Le
Jour des cadeaux', where he describes the unheroic nature of his
faith, and compares his contribution as being:

Quelque chose d'affreux et de compliqué,
Où il a mis tout son cœur et qui ne sert à quoi que ce soit . . .

Like the present his little daughter, 'le cœur gonflé d'orgueil et de
timidité', brought to him on his birthday: 'Un magnifique petit
canard, œuvre de ses mains, pour y mettre des épingles en laine
rouge et en fil doré'.

Claudel's theatre, then, is the main part of his output, on which
his fame rests; the lyric poetry, despite individual examples such
as I have just given, remains far behind. What is surprising and
impressive is the scope and excellence of his prose work, from all
stages of his life. This has now been made available to all by the new
edition in the Bibliothèque de la Pléiade, with notes by Jacques
Petit and Charles Galpérine. It is a great regret to me that we have
no study in this volume of this fascinating part of Claudel's work.

Claudel was not just a dramatic poet; he was also very much
concerned with the details of the production of his plays; indeed
far more so than is usually realized. Annie Barnes's article in this
volume gives us new documentary evidence with regard to the
production of *L'Annonce faite à Marie* at Hellerau just before the
First World War, and makes Claudel's intentions of that time
clear. What is fascinating is to realize the gulf between most
modern productions and these intentions of the author, as is clear
also from Michael Wood's study of *Le Soulier de satin*.

What has been said so far has been aimed at producing an

untrammelled view of Claudel as an *author*, and at freeing him from those overtones which turn people away from him. Claudel is a great author; but, as in the case of most great authors, we can, even if unconcerned at this point with artistic criteria, find things in him which are of great interest. The social historian, the ecclesiologist, can find much to interest them here, and rightly so, as long as historical and religious criteria are not taken to create literary excellence on their own, and so long as the author is not judged solely by them. Like many authors of any significance Claudel is a witness to his age, and valuable to any assessment of trends of thought in that period.

Any history of Catholic thought in the years between the Franco-Prussian War and the First World War in France will find in Claudel a typical example of many of the tendencies of the time. In his violence in relation to the supposed enemies of his faith, and in the many exaggerations of his approach to the mysteries of that faith, he was very much a man of his generation, full of heroism and devotion to a harsh religion which to many people must seem an exaggeration and distortion of Catholic belief, but which is perfectly understandable when taken in relation to the various stresses which were affecting French Catholicism at the time, both in temporal and spiritual matters.

Such essays as Patrick McCarthy's article in this volume not only give us insight into religious attitudes of the time (and in this specific instance, the relation between certain ideas of English Catholicism and those of Paul Claudel), but also tend to clarify even further, for students of Claudel's plays, certain tendencies of his thought with relation to love, renunciation and discipline, just those things which we have seen to have such an effect upon the themes of his plays.

Other articles which, as well as helping us towards a further understanding of the plays, also give us insight into some of the tendencies of contemporary religious thought as they are reflected in these works, include Moya Laverty's study of *Jeanne d'Arc au bûcher*, and Ernest Beaumont's chapter on 'Claudel and Sophia'. Literary affinities are explored in Professor Gilbert Gadoffre's

'Claudel and Balzac', iconographic evidence in Jean Mouton's 'Albums of Paul Claudel'. The important influence of Poland on Claudel is shown to us not only by Witold Leitgeber's fascinating article, but also by a text from Claudel's own hand, hitherto unpublished. And we finish the volume with a study by a scholar resident in France, Prince Alexander Mavrocordato, of a text written by Claudel in the English language.

The works of Paul Claudel have not so far achieved much in the way of popularity in England. Why is this so? On the whole, for the same kinds of reason that have made him unpopular in certain areas of French thought; it is merely that in England we have less of those political and religious groups, which make up a great deal of his support in France. As I have said, the prevalence of the use of criteria other than aesthetic in order to judge the man's works is probably as much the fault of his admirers as of anyone else; but those who object to Claudel on these grounds are themselves to blame as well. An objector to Claudel who bases his judgment of this author on aesthetic grounds, or on grounds which actually have bearing on the effectiveness of the plays, is at least an honest objector, and a man whose criticisms must be taken seriously. But such people are rare. Far more common is the kind of criticism which bases itself on extraneous matters.

One of the most common forms that this takes is that of anti-Catholicism, at its extreme the unreasoning kind of anti-Catholicism which has been described as having become the anti-semitism of the liberal intellectual. Admittedly, as we have seen, the admirers of Claudel have laid themselves open to this danger through over-stressing, and at times over-sentimentalizing, the importance of the Catholic content of Claudel's works. But much of the violence with which this is used to damn these works shows that Claudel's opponents are committing the same fault. While such violence on the part of traditional opponents of Catholicism is only to be expected, it is however, distressing to see many people of moderation taking the views of both admirers and critics as being true, and believing that Claudel, because he is a

'Catholic' author, cannot be for them. Neglecting to look at him purely as an author, without this *parti pris*, they presume that his work is limited in this way, and is not for them. They do not condemn, they merely avoid.

As a corollary to this, many people believe that Claudel's political views are an equally good reason for disliking his works. They see him as a man of the Right, a man who supported Franco in the Spanish Civil War, a man believing in political order and discipline, and opposed to most of what the Left of his day has stood for. In this they would be right. And so the Left condemn his plays, on which these ideas of his have little bearing. It would be as just for a Catholic to condemn the plays of Shakespeare because the author was believed to have been one of Walsingham's spies. I have heard people say that they 'find it impossible to read Claudel, because of his detestable political ideas'.

Of course, if one's political or religious opinions differ from Claudel's, it is perfectly justifiable to criticize him in a purely political or religious context, as did John Weightman recently when, referring to General de Gaulle, he said: 'I, for one, find his absolute nationalism similar to, and as detestable as, Léon Bloy's or Paul Claudel's absolute Catholicism' (*Observer Review*, 7 January 1968). Many people would question the comparison, and many others might prefer Claudel's political and religious views to whatever views Mr Weightman himself holds, but Mr Weightman is at least on the right court here, and is not using Claudel's views to damn him *as an artist*.

A third reason for some people's rejection of Claudel is their impression of him as a person. Here again, of course, it has been a dangerous move on the part of his admirers to stress so much how admirable he was as a person. Hagiography has its dangers; and it does not need the qualities of a Lytton Strachey to see through much of the Claudel cult. While, like all men, he must have had many redeeming qualities, it is nevertheless very clear, from many contemporary descriptions and, indeed, from his own interviews and letters, that he must have been extremely objectionable. Harold Nicolson's impression of him, expressed in a letter to his sons after a meeting in October 1944, is mild compared with that of some people:

> I lunched with Massigli to meet Paul Claudel. . . . Claudel is not an attractive man, being senile and leery and a trifle mean. . . . He was *not* a nice man, and he spoke in a bad way about Gide, saying that his exposure of his own vices reminded him of the monkeys on Monkey Hill, *faisant des obscénités avec une triste dignité*, and he was disagreeable about everyone else.

Disagreeable Claudel may have been, but if one is to believe Jean Dutourd in his study of Claudel in *Les Taxis de la Marne*, it is one of the concomitants of greatness to be *déplaisant*. Certainly there is more evidence of this than of the opposite. Claudel was perpetually aware of his own shortcomings in this respect, and would use the same terms of himself as his critics did: pharisaical, hard, angry, full of rigidity. His awareness of these faults is honest and impressive; and his explanation for some of them is convincing . Claudel was, in a sense, a man living outside his own generation. He had outlived his true contemporaries, those hard Catholics, many of whom died in the First World War, and who had reacted violently in their day against the very real dangers attacking their Church. They had gone to extremes, but so had their enemies; and when we look at these men now it is in no sense of condemnation. Claudel, on the other hand, is so near to us in time that we cannot obtain the same unbiased vision, nor forget the man's personality. He was unable to adapt himself, in the sense that he took the same attitudes, in a very different situation where the Church and its supporters no longer had to fear the unbridled enmity of others, as he had before 1914, when it seemed necessary to be absolute in one's judgments, and *vae tepidis*. We can condone, or even forget, the violence and injustice of many of Péguy's opinions, because he is far enough away from us. But we seem unable to ignore the violence and injustice of Claudel, even though this has no real bearing on his dramatic work.

So the three things which appear to me to lead to unjustified judgments about Claudel's work are opinions as to his religion, his politics, and his personality. These are common both to England and France. There is, however, one other thing which appears to weight the balance against this author in England, which is in a sense justifiable, and which in part explains why a smaller proportion of the educated public read him here than in France. This is the problem of the poet's chosen form of expression.

The French language is far more suited than English to rhetorical effects such as Claudel achieves in his verse. Not only the nature of the language itself, but also the literary taste of the inhabitants of the country. And while a great many people in England have, through their other contacts with French literature, and through their appreciation of the particular virtues of the French language itself, come to admire the Claudelian style, and to place it high in their scale of estimation, there are many others who, having to read his works in translation, find the unaccustomed atmosphere particularly oppressive. The translator's job is an extremely difficult one, as he has to try to transfer the feeling of a Claudel passage into English, while at the same time attempting to make it conform to acceptable English usage. What is remarkable is the amount of outstanding success that has been achieved in this most difficult of exercises.

Claudel still, however, remains an author who has not made a large impression upon English taste. It has been the intention of the writers in this volume, all of them Claudel admirers, to attempt to show some of the reasons for their enthusiasm, and perhaps to convert one or two more people to an appreciation of the author who has aroused it, an author of whose greatness they are in no doubt.

Part one · A new view of some of
Claudel's works

2 · The enigma of *Partage de midi:* a study in ambiguity

BERNARD HOWELLS

Fata volentem ducent – Seneca

ALL OF CLAUDEL'S WORK can be read as an attempt to integrate the two moral personalities which inhabited him and between which the points of difference were more important than the similarities: the Romantic Idealist and the Christian. Most of what we find in the plays, in particular the confusions, the ambiguities and the contradictions can be traced back to the interference of one of these personalities with the other. The development of the plays as a whole shows the gradual overcoming (never completed) of the Romantic by the Christian, and nowhere are the differences between the two kinds of spirituality more apparent than in the Romantic and the Christian attitudes towards evil, and in the set of assumptions either holds about the status of passion. The Romantic attitude to evil can be broadly termed 'fatalistic' in that the self is considered pure, and responsibility for evil is thrown off either on to the metaphysical structure of existence (those philosophical dualisms which see the human spirit as imprisoned in a world which is not God though it might at times offer a tantalizing image of God), or on to an external agent (God, identified Jansenistically with Fate and leaving room only for that residual or phantasmal form of responsibility which is the sense of guilt). For the Christian the natural unregenerate self is evil and responsible; creation *taken as a whole* is good and God is the author of this goodness. So that we find in the early 'trilogy' (*Tête d'or*, *La Ville*, *Le Repos du septième jour*) a poetry of malediction, coming from an asphyxiating feeling of imprisonment in contingency, coexisting with a lyrical sense of the beauty and goodness of creation which at moments offers hints of transcendental release; protestations of self-justification along-side intuitions of personal guilt and responsibility.

Claudel's task was to transform *la blessure romantique* (the sense of frustration arising from the gap between transcendental desire and the kinds of satisfaction the world has to offer) into the Christian sense of sin and responsibility for evil. In his reflection upon tragic experience he had to come to see that the tragic flaw was not within the structure of existence but within the human conscience. The Romantic Idealist in Claudel was always ready to consider himself more sinned against than sinning. Only very slowly does the Christian idea of personal responsibility for good and evil emerge, introducing a fatal division into the hitherto homogeneous consciousness of the Romantic hero like Simon Agnel or Avare, and modifying the kind of cathartic effect created in the plays.

The plays from *Tête d'or* to *La Jeune Fille Violaine* (2me version) can be taken as a fairly homogeneous unit. They represent what one might call the drama of *Ignorance* because in them Claudel is groping from the Idealist's view of the human condition towards the Christian assumption of destiny by free-will. *Partage de midi*, *L'Annonce*, the Trilogy and *Le Soulier de satin* form a second grouping, based this time on recognition (though at moments this is not without equivocation) of responsibility for salvation and damnation. *Partage de midi* occupies a special place in this development. It is a partial relapse because in it, under the influence of the emotional crisis of 1901–4, the drama of responsibility is attenuated by an attempt to resurrect the Romantic myth of fatal passion which unconsciously pushed Claudel towards a theology of grace and liberty which can only be described as Jansenistic (Mesa sees himself as 'un juste à qui la grâce a manqué'). The play is ambiguous because the 'natural' Romantic side of Claudel's nature is distorting the pattern imposed by religious orthodoxy. It is confused, inconclusive and ultimately, despite the feverish re-handling of the last act, unresolvable because in it Claudel was using two systems of reference to interpret his life-experience. *Partage de midi* is on the one hand a tragedy of frustrated Romantic desire, which tends to fatalism and to exonerate the hero. On the other hand it records clearly the Christian tragedy of a consciousness divided against itself in the knowledge of good and evil. These ambiguities are centred on the character of Mesa. One could object that the mentality of the hero in the play does not necessarily represent the mentality of the author who wrote it. This raises the delicate and involved critical question of the author's distance from the text and his attitude towards it. In Claudel's case there is abundant evidence to suggest that his attitude towards the fundamental ambiguity of *Partage de midi* was itself equivocal. He admitted that the first version was simply 'une espèce d'explosion inconsciente de mes sentiments intérieurs'.[1] Claudel's attitude became more hostile as years passed, but despite, or even because of his vehement protestations of orthodoxy in *Mémoires improvisés* and his harsh strictures against the character of Mesa, equivocation is never totally expulsed.

Partage de midi is the story of a *predestined passion* which leads through *sin* to *salvation* with only a minimal gesture in the direction of *repentance*. This is the pattern established in the first version of the play and it remains, with important modifications, the basis of the subsequent versions. The passion is unequivocally predestined. It is presented by Claudel as being the will of God and is celebrated in a lyricism that draws on all the myths associated with fatal passion in Romantic writing. Notions connected with the Platonic hermaphrodite and the myth of 'l'existence antérieure' proliferate in the last version. The ironical vulgarity with which they, and the character of Mesa, are treated must not mislead the reader. There is no question of ironical detachment here but simply of emotional self-aggression which stiffened as the conviction of predestination hardened in Claudel's mind from version to version. Critics have rightly felt that the quality of the irony clashes with the assumptions latent in the text. A similar kind of aggression made Claudel claim that the final version of the play was technically superior to the first. In actual fact it is not and what he claimed was a technical rehandling was in reality a radical and abortive attempt to modify the play's meaning.

The salvation envisaged, on the other hand, is highly equivocal. In *Partage I* it is a Romantic salvation; a projection beyond the limitations of life of the lovers' yearning for unity. Claudel tries to assimilate this kind of Romantic union into the idea of union with God through the use of scriptural and liturgical references. In the stage versions Act III is tampered with in a rather erratic fashion. The 'salvation' which Providence had in view in allowing this spiritual catastrophe, we are told, was to inculcate into Mesa 'le sentiment de l'Autre' with the assumption that he will, in some mysterious way, lead Ysé too towards salvation. Claudel is trying to turn the Romantic idea of the union of the lovers in death towards more orthodox ends.

Although there are long passages in the 1905 version where both Ysé and Mesa express feelings of remorse and guilt, neither goes through the phase of repentance *in the proper sense of the word* (i.e. a radical re-orientation of the *will* away from the object of adulterous desire), for the simple reason that in Romantic psychology the beauty of Ysé, even within adultery, remains an image of the Divine. Not even in the last versions is there any radical renunciation of the kind we find, according to Jacques Petit, at the end of *Le Soulier de satin*[2]. Indeed, on the contrary, throughout all the versions there persists something of the idea suggested in *Partage I*; De Ciz being dead, the relationship between the lovers is 'regularized' and tensions resolved by a kind of mystical marriage, or mutual 'consentement' as Claudel calls it. This may be another conscious gesture to orthodoxy, but as such it is particularly unconvincing since it has been made clear in the course of the play that what makes it wrong for Mesa to possess Ysé is not so much the formal barrier of marriage but the fact that, as Mesa says, *he loved her too much*. Her possession, even in marriage, would have been exclusive of his love of God. In other words, intense sexual passion for Claudel was not ultimately compatible with religious aspiration, though there was a side of him which wanted to invest sex with all the prestige of religious aspiration. I want to suggest that this drama of *Désir – Interdiction – Consentement devant la mort*, which as consciously presented in the play involves utterly incompatible elements, corresponds in fact to a perfectly coherent and common psychoanalytical pattern in Claudel which could not reach expression without being distorted by the religious writer's ambition to rescue his life from the vagaries of temperament and invest it with permanent meaning.

There remains the question of the lovers' sin, and it is here that the problem of distinguishing between Romantic fatalism and Christian orthodoxy is most acute. Does the lovers' fall form part of the predestined scheme as well as the passion that brought it about? It seems irrelevant to try, as some commentators have done, to dissolve the problem in the doctrine of second causes, i.e. God placed Ysé in Mesa's way in order that he should love her 'at a distance' and somehow bring her soul to salvation. This is perfectly orthodox theology but it has got nothing to do with the play. It is in fact looking at *Partage de midi* with the hindsight afforded by *Le Soulier de satin*. Such a possibility is never presented as a dramatic alternative and is not part of the impact the play produces on us. In fact in his presentation of material the drama of moral choice is deliberately suppressed by Claudel, though the drama of moral division remains. The mainspring of the dramatic tension, especially in Act II, lies in a structure of feelings which Professor Gérald Antoine has compared with those governing *Phèdre*.[3] Within the grip of fatal passion Mesa preserves a heightened sense of good and evil. But his sense of guilt and even of willing his own sin never amounts to a genuine assumption of responsibility. His feeling of moral paralysis is identical to that expressed by Claudel in the letters to Suarès. The seeming paradox in the dilemma portrayed is only explicable in terms of a tacit theology whose implications are Jansenistic. We are here dealing with an awareness of freedom which is clearly not awareness of autonomy exercised in choice. It is merely freedom to espouse whichever of the two 'délectations' makes itself felt most strongly. To this answers a conception of a transcendent force which moves man, if not by an absolute necessity, then at least by a 'nécessité d'infaillibilité'. Jansenism is the only point where compromise is possible between Romantic fatalism and Christian responsibility by a modification of both elements and it tends to occur in Romantic writing whenever the Romantic attitude to evil tries to put on a Christian garb over its Manichaean or neo-Platonic one. It would be patently absurd to claim that Claudel was a Jansenist and that therefore the story of sinful passion in *Partage de midi* took the form it did. Rather the contrary; Claudel's experience of Romantic fatal passion, when he tried to fit it into a Christian scheme of things, led him into a borderline theology of grace and liberty which he would have consciously repudiated. What made the distortion possible was a set of sophistical assumptions at the heart of Romanticism concerning the nature of passion and its relation to the soul's love of God. One might add that whilst it is impossible to attach the formal label of tragedy to *Partage de midi* except by ignoring the last act, one can talk about 'l'expression du tragique' in connection with the play. The tragic finds a mode of entry in so far as the play portrays a certain view of human liberty in relation to a transcendent force where the two are not categorically opposed, as they are in discursive philosophy, but where fate becomes interiorized to the point of being inseparable from human volition, in a kind of mysterious *amor fati*.[4]

The ambiguities sketched out above, Claudel's attempts to push the final versions of the play towards a moralistic ending despite the natural resistance of the material out of which it is made, suggest that he never became really clear-sighted about his experience. The play for this reason is a critic's nightmare but one which tells us a lot about Claudel's psyche. Ernest Beaumont took up Claudel's invitation to read coherence into the play by interpreting it through the myth of Beatrice. His conclusion was that *Partage* is 'the most audacious variation that the French poet has contrived on the theme of Beatrice and one of the least satisfactory'.[5] The truth is that the Beatrician myth of an unfulfilled love whose aspirations are dissolved in the mysticism of a future union beyond death, vague in nature and indefinitely postponed, represents only as much of the Romantic fatal passion myth as Claudel would allow to filter through into his conscious way of thinking. What really underlies *Partage de midi* is the Tristan myth of a fiercely sexual passion that aspires to death.[6] It is no coincidence that from about 1910 onwards Claudel's enthusiasm for Wagner deteriorated into revulsion directed primarily at the 'lugubre immoralité de Tristan, et du couple incestueux de la Walküre'.[7] In rejecting 'le poison wagnérien' Claudel was resisting his own complicity with a certain toxic quality of sexual feeling.

The ambiguity of *Partage de midi* where the question of liberty and predestination is concerned is best seen in the divergent views of two 1948 commentators who looked at the text through the lens of their own respective philosophies of life and art. In general Gabriel Marcel criticized Claudel for a type of dogmatic theology which might have been possible in the age of Dante but which was incompatible with the modern mentality. For Marcel the play is moving because it is a record of a man's free acts. The element of fatalism in the Marigny version comes from a heavy-handed *a posteriori* interpretation foisted on to the play in Act III and in the preface, and which implies an unacceptable view of human liberty in relation to providential purpose.[8] François Mauriac, on the other hand, confessed that *Partage* caused him to 'rêver dangereusement aux confins de l'hérésie'.[9] He specifically connects the conviction of predetermination with Port-Royal and with *Phèdre*, making the distinction however that here we are dealing with a predestination through grace to salvation and not with a fatality through the natural order to damnation.[10] It would seem then that the only way to approach a play like *Partage de midi* or *Le Soulier de satin*, where the dramatist's intentions are not clear to himself, is to follow the example of M. Petit in refusing to be put off by the ambiguities and the blatant contradictions, and to cut through the tangle of luxuriant lyricism till one finds the conviction, felt rather than formulated, out of which the play springs and of which it is a *more or less faithful* elaboration. Lyrical poetry in Claudel's drama fulfils the ambiguous role of what psychologists call the 'screen-image'. Its first function is self-expression leading to self-knowledge. Its second function is to prevent some aspects of that self-knowledge from being brought to clear consciousness; in Claudel's case a consciousness patterned by

Christian orthodoxy. In *Partage de midi* Claudel was trying to give a complex set of instinctual impulses some kind of conscious, religious meaning. We can expect to find a great deal of mutual interference between self-expression and formulated meaning, just as, at the origin of the play, we find an emotional conviction acknowledged with an intellectual equivocation:

> J'ai eu le sentiment, et bien fort, que ce ne pouvait pas être autrement. Ysé, *le Partage de midi*, et dans quelles conditions les choses se sont passées, humainement, il était presque impossible qu'elles tournent autrement. Tout semblait réuni pour ça. J'ai d'ailleurs eu le sentiment que j'étais garrotté, que j'étais pris dans une espèce de guet-apens d'où il était impossible de m'échapper. *Le Partage de midi* en dit plus long là-dessus que je ne pourrais vous l'expliquer.[11]

The overpowering conviction is one of a predestination that includes the passion, the sin and the final outcome. 'Humainement presque impossible' is a gesture to orthodoxy; equivocal, because in acknowledging the reality of grace it implies that this grace in the event was not forthcoming.

How did this sense of predetermination in connection with sexual passion come to enter into Claudel's way of feeling and from there into his way of thinking? Through his boyhood and adolescent reading of Romantic, Symbolist and Decadent literature, the assumptions of the Romantic outlook, the myths and patterns in which its erotic sensibility expressed itself, its ambivalent attitude, in the literature of the end of the century, towards sensuality and sexuality; all these elements entered into Claudel's unconscious way of thinking and there linked up with personal myths that were forming out of the structure of feelings which his own sexual impulse was setting up inside him.

It would be naïve to imagine that the conflict between Claudel's will to self-domination and his temperamental inclinations began only with his conversion and had no psychological pre-history. Fr. Varillon has shown, with reference to *L'Endormie* and *Fragment d'un drame*, how, early on, the sexual drive in Claudel became polarized into a system of idealization and a system of degradation (*Galaxaure* and *Strombo* of *L'Endormie*).[12] 'Idealization' may be thought of as a set of feelings which would commonly pass for love, though they can only be entertained upon the tacit assumption that consummation is impossible. 'Degradation', more commonly thought of as hate, springs paradoxically from an aggressive fear of the crudity and violence of carnal experience secretly desired. More important than the poet's bivalent imaginings in *L'Endormie* is Claudel's aggression towards his own erotic daydreams; an aggression born out of fear of the strength of his own impulses and reinforced by a sense of guilt bound up with inadmissible feelings of incest and parricide. Put more simply: Claudel possessed a high degree of libido and an equally strong repression mechanism. In the absence of any contact with women outside his own family these turned inward and set up a double-sighted attitude towards sexuality; a desire to enjoy, yet a censoring of this desire – a *désir* and an *interdiction*. 'La thématique de la femme inaccessible', as Varillon calls it,[13] expresses this double-sightedness which persisted throughout Claudel's life and gives rise to some of the most striking emotional and moral paradoxes in the plays.

How things happened on board the *Ernest-Simons* we shall never know. What matters is that in the play the real-life experience has been imaginatively recreated in a 'mythical' kind of writing which sorts out the most significant elements in that experience. The structure of the play is built around a set of responses between Ysé and Mesa which can be described through a number of formulas taken from the text and which will be seen to fall into a psychoanalytical pattern that does a lot to clarify the confused data of the writing. Firstly the mysterious 'recognition' between Mesa and Ysé from which the play proceeds. This is cleverly preceded in the text by the purely 'natural' recognition between Ysé and Amalric, and when it does take place there is a distinct break and a change in the pitch of the dialogue. As in the scene of avowal between Phèdre and Hippolyte; this simple dramatic device is used to indicate that we are dealing with unconscious utterances which Ysé a few moments later recognizes as such. The suggestion that this is a relationship formed in an undefined past or at another level of existence, lost then refound, makes it more than plausible to suggest that the 'recognition' is in fact the 'recovery' of an 'archaeological' situation, the projection on to Ysé of a suppressed pattern of sexual feelings in Claudel. What Claudel/Mesa 'recognizes' in Ysé is a correspondence of the patterns governing sexuality in his own psyche. In this sense Ysé is quite literally, as Mesa claims her to be, the 'key' to his soul and therefore to his destiny. The series of definitions she gives of herself are always definitions of Mesa's feelings towards her. She is *désirable* and *interdite* precisely to the extent that sex for Claudel had been a matter of *désir* and *interdiction*. She is *l'impossible* not because she is married (she insists that even if she were free she would not consent to marry Mesa), but because Mesa is *afraid of loving her too much*. Fear of the Dionysian side of his own nature was one of the reasons which led to Claudel's attempt to give up literature and enter Ligugé in 1900. Mesa's inability to 'give himself' in guilty passion is given as the reason for the failure of the relationship in the play and one must always bear in mind that, as in *Phèdre*, the real sense of guilt is attached not so much to the legal obstacle as to the incoercible violence of the passion itself. Even before the actual adultery Mesa recognizes clearly that a woman loved passionately must always be for him 'Celle qui est à la place du bonheur', and that he turned to religion as an excuse for his inability to give himself over unreservedly to the kind of drive, particularly the sexual drive, that takes us into the created world:

> Il faudrait se donner à elle tout entier!
> Et il n'y a absolument pas moyen, et à quoi est-ce que cela
>   servirait?
> Il n'y a pas moyen de vous donner mon âme,
> Ysé.
> C'est pourquoi je me suis tourné d'un autre côté.[14]

It is the awareness of this inability which kills the relationship before it starts; but the point is that Mesa *wants* to kill it and can only enter into the experience of passion on the condition there is no possibility of a permanent human commitment. The fact that Ysé is *impossible* is the most important definition of her nature in Mesa's eyes. It is ultimately the condition of his love for her and that love derives its intensity from the fascination of the taboo. It is clear from the text that the passion of Ysé and Mesa is held in being by the very tensions implicit in it and that it was engendered in the first place by those same tensions. Before the 'recognition' we are told that Ysé is afraid of Mesa's moral judgment of her and Mesa in turn is fascinated and dismayed by Ysé's coquettish sensuality and moral instability.

What there is of resolution in the last act seems to hinge upon the idea of *consentement devant la mort* which is attenuated in the last version to a simple mutual acceptance and forgiveness but which is still there. At a conscious level this is viewed ambiguously by Claudel; as the condition either of a Romantic apotheosis of love, or of Christian absolution and hope of future redemption. The important thing to note is that there *is* a genuine resolution of dramatic tension in so far as there is a radical change of feeling where the relationship of Mesa and Ysé is concerned. 'Tout est devenu vrai' as Ysé says.[15] A psychological 'regularization' has taken place which is more significant than the pseudo-legal one. The lovers individually still express feelings of guilt and remorse for the past but the sense of guilt in the relationship itself has now disappeared (and with it has gone the need for any real repentance). The continuing love between Ysé and Mesa is no longer felt as an obstacle to salvation but as a means of salvation and the symbols used in Acts II and III to express the moral quality of this love (the *omega* for instance) have also subtly reversed meaning to answer this new conviction. In short the element of *interdiction* has gone from the relationship and it has gone because the relationship has no proper human future. Consent to each other is possible because fulfilment is impossible. The lovers can entertain their feelings without remorse in the face of death because death is what makes them definitively inaccessible to each other. What has created this new psychological situation is the break which Mesa indirectly forced Ysé into making, especially after he learned she was pregnant. Mesa rejects the child as a symbol of permanence in a passionate sexual relationship, just as he rejects Ysé herself. Even though he might afterwards want her and the child back, to the point of considering himself betrayed by Ysé, this apparently positive element in his feeling can only be entertained because the situation is fundamentally irretrievable. Dr Beaumont was right to suggest that there is more than a hint of infanticide in *Partage I*.[16] The child of consummated desire dies (in *Partage* and *L'Annonce*). Only the child of unconsummated love ('l'enfant par l'esprit'), to whom there is attached no sense of guilt, can be allowed to live (*L'Annonce* and *Le Soulier*).

In the absence of any proper integration between sexuality and the religious ideal, Claudel had two ways of coming to terms with the conflict between them; one in life, the other in literature. In the first place he tried through marriage to incorporate his relationship with woman into an ascetical view of spirituality. The 'maison fermée' of conjugal life was, as Richard Griffiths has pointed out, Claudel's substitute for the monastic 'clôture'.[17] Marriage was good for Claudel less as a form of sexual fulfilment than as a way of keeping the flesh at bay. On the other hand he tried, through poetry, to turn sexuality into a form of religious aspiration. This was the only solution his confused mind could see in 1905 and it produced Act III of the first version of *Partage de midi*. What made this assimilation possible was a psychology of passion which, paradoxically and with very different emphasis, the Romantics shared with Jansenism.

What Claudel objected to in Jansenism, particularly in later life, was its association with purely negative theology, i.e. the tendency to see God and the world as irreconcilable opposites; and the drive that takes us towards them as moving in opposite directions; the direction determining whether the drive is to be considered good or evil. In this scheme of things created beauty cannot be considered an image of the Divine, in any direct sense, only an unsatisfactory alternative to it. This is Mesa's frame of mind in Act II of *Partage de midi*. For the reasons already suggested, Claudel's belief in positive transcendental passion was able to reassert itself in Act III. What, we must then ask ourselves, is the assumption common to these two different modes in which love is felt and imagined? Stated simply: for Claudel the Romantic, as for the author of the 18th *Lettre Provinciale*, it is fundamentally the same drive, the same kind of impassioned feeling that takes us towards God as towards woman. Claudel was fond of applying to *Partage de midi* Lacordaire's formula 'il n'y a pas deux amours'. The difference between the Romantic Idealist and the Jansenist is that for the former woman and God lie in the same plane with respect to the drive and one has to be transcended to get to the other. For the latter God and created beauty are opposite poles of solicitation; there is no question of transcending the loved object, only of conversion from it. But where Claudel (and Romanticism as a whole) came together again with Jansenism was in abolishing the traditional moral distinction between two kinds of orientation towards a love-object: impassioned feeling and voluntary aspiration; want and will. On the level of theoretical psychology there may be certain difficulties raised by postulating the existence in man of two wills; but on the other hand the attempt to heal over this split in consciousness to an extent which effectively removes creative control over one's destiny opened wide the doors to sophistry, and through them the conviction of fatality flooded into Claudel's thinking, forced there by the accumulated psychological pressures described above. It was this kind of unconscious sophistry where the status of passion is concerned which enabled Claudel in Act III of *Partage de midi* to hold up adulterous passion as a form of the soul's longing for God. More important than that; it enables the Mesa of Act II to experience all the anguish of remorse and guilt without ever really acknowledging responsibility.

It seems to me, as far as *Partage de midi* is concerned, difficult to counter the accusation that Claudel is projecting into his conception of providential purpose the secret wishes of his own unconscious and that this led him, almost inevitably, into a kind of fatalism in Christian disguise, where the problem of evil is virtually dissolved in the notion of final causes. The fatalism is of a borderline variety and has a very respectable literary history. The optimism is of a Romantic kind even though it might have been culled from sources as diverse as St Augustine, Bossuet and Joseph de Maistre. The portrayal of human freedom in relation to sin and to salvation in *Partage* implies a view of efficacious grace, withdrawn then restored to make good triumph. As long as Claudel remained within the magnetic field of *Partage de midi* he could never eliminate completely the elements of the Romantico-Jansenist sophistry from the text. He finally had to write them out of his system in an entirely new play which, throughout its long length, struggles to get beyond equivocation and finally does so though not without leaving the text littered with the broken evidence of ambiguity. *Le Soulier de satin* ultimately does come down on the side of Transcendence grasped through sacrifice rather than through desire, and there is, as M. Petit points out, a ritualistic burning of some elements of the Romantic myth through the character of Don Camille.[18] I would add that it also comes down on the side of sufficient grace and a view of human liberty equally more acceptable. The dramatic irony of the play is centred around the gift of the slipper and the important 'theological' scene in the 3me *Journée* with the Guardian Angel. Prouhèze invokes the help of grace by trying to slough off her liberty; only to find that the way grace really operates is to prize her sufficiently free of concupiscence to make her aware of her liberty and of the alternatives between which it has to choose. We have left behind the drama of Compulsion and entered the drama of Persuasion.

NOTES

1. *Mémoires improvisés*, Paris: Gallimard, 1954, p. 188.
2. Jacques Petit, *Pour une explication du 'Soulier de satin'*, Paris: Archives des Lettres Modernes No. 58, 1965.
3. Gérald Antoine, 'L'Expression du tragique dans *Partage de midi*' in *Le Théâtre tragique*, Paris: Editions du Centre National de la Recherche Scientifique, 1962.
4. See Jacques Madaule, 'Le Tragique chez Claudel' in *Le Théâtre tragique*.

5. Ernest Beaumont, *The Theme of Beatrice in the Plays of Claudel*, London: Rockliff, 1954, p. 43.

6. See the suggestive article by Jacques Duron, 'Le Mythe de Tristan', *Hommage à Paul Claudel, NRF*, Sept. 1955.

7. 'Le Poison wagnérien', *Contacts et circonstances*, Paris: Gallimard, 1947, p. 136.

8. Gabriel Marcel, 'Partage de midi', *Les Nouvelles littéraires*, No. 1113, 30.12.1948.

9. François Mauriac, *Réponse à Paul Claudel* (Académie française, séance du 13.3.1947), Paris: Editions de la Table Ronde, 1947, p. 48.

10. 'Note sur *Partage de midi*', *Mercure de France*, mai-août 1948, pp. 5–6.

11. *Mémoires improvisés*, p. 182.

12. François Varillon, *Claudel*, (Les écrivains devant Dieu), Paris: Desclée de Brouwer, 1967.

13. ibid., p. 81.

14. 1ʳᵉ version, *Théâtre, I*, Pl., Paris, 1956, p. 1003.

15. ibid., p. 1055.

16. op. cit., p. 37.

17. Richard Griffiths, *The Reactionary Revolution*, London: Constable, 1966, pp. 323–5.

18. op. cit., pp. 25, 45–54.

3 · *L'Annonce faite à Marie* at Hellerau (October 1913)

ANNIE BARNES

For Egon Wellesz

BETWEEN 1909 and 1911, at Tientsin and then at Prague, *La Jeune Fille Violaine* became *L'Annonce faite à Marie*. The *Nouvelle Revue Française* published the Prologue and the first Act in its December number 1911, and then Acts II, III, and IV between January and March 1912. From October 1911 onwards Claudel was Consul-General at Frankfurt, and it was from Frankfurt that he went to Paris in October 1912 for the rehearsals of *L'Annonce* at the Théâtre de l'Oeuvre. Thanks to a public consisting above all of young people, the three performances at the end of December were a great success. In the review he wrote for the *NRF*, however, Jean Schlumberger was to express certain reservations: 'Ce n'est pas que de premier coup, l'interprétation ait atteint cette simplicité et cette grandeur qu'on est en droit d'exiger.'[1] Less than a year later, however, the play was to know simplicity and grandeur such as Schlumberger had desired, when Jakob Hegner's translation was performed at the theatre of Hellerau on 5, 11, and 19 October 1913.

The publisher Jakob Hegner, who was a fervent admirer of Claudel, settled at Hellerau in 1912 in order to devote himself to the translation and publication of the works of the French poet. Under the title of *Verkündigung*, his translation of *L'Annonce faite à Marie* appeared in 1912, only a few months after the original edition in France; and the following year two more editions were to appear.

'Sur la colline au-dessus de Dresde, au milieu des bois de pins'[2] the garden city of Hellerau, founded in 1911 by architects, artists, writers and craftsmen, had become by 1913 a flourishing community of two thousand inhabitants. Its experimental theatre, whose main organizer was the French Swiss composer Jaques-Dalcroze, the creator of eurhythmics, had gained an international reputation. Max Reinhardt, Nijinsky, Stanislavsky, G. B. Shaw, Upton Sinclair, all came to initiate themselves into the method and to attend the performances.

In view of the presence of Hegner at Hellerau, and of the excellent terms on which he was with the Consul-General at Frankfurt, it was natural that the play *Verkündigung* should have been put on the programme of the *Festspiele* in 1913. We know that Claudel was at Hellerau in June to supervise the first rehearsals of *L'Annonce*. It was on that occasion that he attended a performance of Gluck's *Orfeo* given by Dalcroze's pupils; this performance was a revelation to him. (*Orfeo* with its ballet of the blessed spirits and its dance of the Furies might well have been composed specially for Jaques-Dalcroze's eurhythmics.) On 1 September 1913, the *NRF* published anonymously a letter by Claudel about *Le Théâtre d'Hellerau* which begins as follows:

On va voir deux choses à Hellerau:
1. La musique en des corps humains devenue visible et vivante.
[A page follows, analysing Dalcroze's eurhythmics.]
2. La Salle.
La salle de Hellerau, construite et aménagée par un artiste de génie, M. de Salzmann (Russe) . . .

Claudel then goes on to describe the vast rectangle, which included nothing in the way of a fixed stage setting.

Les parois et le plafond sont faits d'étoffe blanche derrière laquelle sont disposées régulièrement des herses de lampes électriques. Aucun foyer de lumière nue n'est visible . . . Au lieu du feu brutal de la rampe qui colle à plat les acteurs contre la toile de fond et fait de tout tableau un chromo à la fois décoloré et criard, c'est une espèce d'ambiance laiteuse, d'atmosphère élyséenne, qui rend à la troisième dimension son honneur méprisé, et fait de tout corps une statue, dont les plans, les ombres et les reliefs s'accusent et se modèlent comme sous les doigts d'un parfait artiste . . .[3]

Claudel's enthusiasm was not without its drawbacks for the producer of *L'Annonce*. Up till this moment the work had proceeded according to the stage directions printed in the edition, in all their realism and detail. Now the poet wanted to eliminate any scenery which might give the illusion of reality. All this delayed the performance. We know what the new staging was like, from the review *Les 'Festspiele' d'octobre à Hellerau* which Darius Milhaud sent to the *NRF*.

L'installation matérielle de cette scène sur trois plans superposés permet au public de voir simultanément plusieurs motifs du drame: ainsi au quatrième acte, on voit en bas une cavité sombre où se trouve le tombeau de Violaine; au-dessus, sur un second plan, sont Jacques Hury, Mara, Anne Vercors et Pierre de Craon, et au-dessus encore, sur un troisième plan, on voit à la fin apparaître Violaine, vêtue d'or et voilée, encadrée par une sorte d'ogive lumineuse.

La mise en scène a été réglée avec le plus grand soin par Paul Claudel lui-même, aidé du Dr Wolf Dohrn, qui est si dévoué à toutes les manifestations artistiques de Hellerau. L'interprétation a été excellente: on a particulièrement admiré Mlle Mary Dietrich du 'Deutsches Theater' de Berlin, qui a joué le rôle de Mara avec beaucoup de jeunesse et de spontanéité.[4]

For his part Claudel had written to André Gide on 22 September 1913: 'J'ai pour Mara une actrice admirable qui a des détentes de panthère, "la Dietrich".'[5]

Though contemporary accounts are numerous, they tell us little about anything except the setting and the absence of scenery in the Hellerau *Annonce*. A hitherto unpublished document will, however, furnish us with supplementary information. This document is the German text of the play which served as *Regiebuch* (producer's copy) for the production,[6] and which reveals the close collaboration which existed between Claudel, Jakob Hegner, and most probably Wolf Dohrn, producer and Secretary-General of the Hellerau Association.

This *Regiebuch* is a copy of the second edition of *Verkündigung*

(Hellerauer Verlag, 1913). In page-setting and the choice of type, Hegner has reproduced very closely the appearance of the little *NRF* edition. His translation may certainly be considered too free, but it is true to the Claudelian *verset*, to its music and its rhythm.[7] There is one striking error of translation in the Prologue: replying to Pierre de Craon who has gravely said to her 'Mais Justice est une grande pierre elle-même', Violaine said, laughing: 'Je ne suis pas de la même carrière', and Hegner translates this as: 'Ihre Laufbahn ist nicht die meine' (p. 23). A little before this, the 'bosquet de sureaux' has become a 'Fliederbusch' (p. 18), but this is perhaps for reasons of rhythm.

The most striking characteristic of Hegner's translation is that everything which is specifically French in *L'Annonce*, whether it be names of people, names of places, topography or history, everything has been transposed and Germanized. Anne Vercors has become Andreas Gradherz, Andrew of the upright heart, and Pierre de Craon, Peter von Ulm. The numerous cathedrals of France mentioned in the text have easily been provided with their equivalents: Speier, Worms, Köln, Mainz. Monsanvierge is Marienberg, Combernon Salhof, Chevoche Rothenstein. 'Compère loriot! qui mange les cesses et laisse le noyau', which is sung in the first act – as in *La Jeune Fille Violaine* – by a child's voice, is perfectly naturally transformed into 'Kuckuck, Kuckuck! Ruft aus dem Wald!' (p. 62), and the child's voice at the end replaces the folk song 'Marguerite de Paris' with a lullaby of equally popular origin:

Joseph, liebster Joseph mein,
Ach hilf mir wiegen mein Kindelein . . . (p. 186)

The public at Hellerau was also able to appreciate the exclamation of Peter von Ulm which transforms Violaine, the lark of France, into 'Lerche du vom Rhein!' (O lark of the Rhine!) (p. 27). But two pages of the first scene of Act III presented difficulties for the translator which he did not fully succeed in resolving; they are those where the people of Chevoche describe the Maid conducting King Charles to Rheims. Hegner gave up the idea of translating them, and replaced Claudel's text with two pages of his own invention, in which the people of Rothenstein speak of a certain Hans who is conducting King Konrad to Speier. If Claudel's Middle Ages are 'la fin d'un moyen âge de convention', those of his translator are even more vague.

All these changes, we are told, have been made with the author's consent. The document we have before us furnishes the proof of this: although the cuts made to the text are very numerous in it, almost all the passages that have just been mentioned, even the Führer Hans and his King Konrad in Act Three, remain. That is not what interested Claudel.

The *Regiebuch* is marked and annotated in three ways: in red crayon, in ink, and in pencil. The notes in the margin or between the lines reveal three distinct handwritings. Everything in red crayon is by Claudel; Hegner is the only one to write in ink; both of these writers also write in pencil, as does the third annotator, who is probably Wolf Dohrn.

From the appearance of the volume it would seem that Claudel at first worked alone. Armed with a thick red crayon, he made the first cuts, where each line of the text that is to be cut out is crossed out by a thick stroke which one would be tempted to call brutal, and which is in great contrast with the small, fine handwriting of the poet at this time. On two occasions we come across this familiar handwriting, in the margin in places where the red crayon, indicating a change of mind, has traced, with a lightness of which one would not have believed it capable, the word *bleibt* (stet). Occasionally, losing his patience, Claudel crosses out the rest of the text that is to be cut out with an enormous vertical or transversal stroke. These first cuts are few in number; about thirty, unequally distributed. Acts I to III have remained almost intact, while the prologue and the last Act have been relieved of a good deal of the long speeches of Pierre de Craon and of those of Anne Vercors after his return from his pilgrimage. Claudel, who had written to Jacques Rivière in 1909, after having reread *La Jeune Fille Violaine*, that he wanted to 'supprimer les divagations architecturales de la fin',[8] knew that the poet has sometimes to make sacrifices for the benefit of the dramatist.

Jakob Hegner appears to have been the next to read the text, with a pen in his hand. Sometimes, like the gleaner following the harvester, he contents himself with carefully crossing out each line of a passage that has already been indicated for cutting by a great red vertical stroke, sometimes he adds further vertical strokes. But over and above this, he makes many new cuts. It is at this point that the true collaboration begins. One can imagine the poet and his translator, each with a pencil in his hand, discussing the text page by page. New cuts prove necessary from time to time, even in scenes which have up to this point remained un-scathed. But what is above all striking is the number of hesitations and of changes of mind. The three last pages of the prologue (pp. 31–3) which contain no fewer than four crossed-out passages – the first in red crayon, the three others in ink, making in all more than half the text – are entirely restored, thanks to five marginal notes of *bleibt*, the first two and the last one in Claudel's handwriting, the two others in Hegner's.

The same close collaboration is to be seen in the many instruc-tions on the interpretation of the roles. Obviously they are all in German, although it is probable that Claudel and his translator spoke to each other in French. Everything happens as though Hegner had noted Claudel's directives and immediately trans-lated them in the margin of his copy. Indeed, almost all these remarks are in his handwriting, and sometimes a word is crossed out and replaced by another. On a blank page facing the beginning of the text, we read the following:

> Der Prolog soll von der Violäne nicht zu gewichtig, und [corrected to *eher*] heiter gespielt werden, doch aber ernsthaft und mit Bestimmtheit.
>
> Peter von Ulm – rauh, kräftig, feierlich ohne Affektation, zum Schluss in Klängen der Verzweiflung. Er könnte wohl die Silben ein wenig wie hämmernd sprechen.

39

4–C

(In the Prologue Violaine should not play her part in too heavy a manner, but rather in a serene way; nevertheless earnestly and with determination.

Peter von Ulm – rough, strong, dignified without being affected, finally in tones of despair. He might well speak the syllables a little as though hammering them out.)

And when the dialogue starts, Pierre de Craon's speeches twice have the instruction *dumpf* (sombre), and those of Violaine *klar* (clear).

But without following step by step all this work of preparation for the producer, let us note what seems to be of particular interest. Certain of Claudel's instructions certainly seem to go against what we are usually given in French productions. For example as soon as she comes on stage in the first Act (I, ii), Mara reveals her full violence when she twice says to her mother: 'Va, et dis-lui qu'elle ne l'épouse pas'. But here is the Hegner-Claudel commentary on this: 'Mara hält ihre Heimtücke und Heftigkeit zurück. weich, schmeichelnd' (Mara is restraining her malice and her violence. tenderly, wheedling), and, the second time, *weich* (tenderly) again.

The instruction at the beginning of Scene ii, 2, the dialogue between Mara and Jacques, is more what one might expect: 'Mara: deutlich, bewegt, hochmütig, ironisch' (Mara: clear, agitated, arrogant, ironical).

The great scene which follows, between Violaine and Jacques Hury, contains only two such notes. To the cruel words of Jacques: 'Infâme, réprouvée dans ton âme et dans ta chair!' Violaine replies: 'Ainsi vous ne demandez plus à m'épouser, Jacques?' And Hegner notes: 'Violäne stolz und kalt' (Violaine proudly and coldly). This proud and cold Violaine will very soon be transformed, for two pages later, to the question: 'Dites, qu'allez-vous faire, misérable?' she replies: 'Gagner . . . le lieu qui est réservé aux gens de mon espèce. La ladrerie là-bas du Géyn.' And Claudel-Hegner make the comment: 'Ruhig und friedlich' (Quietly and peacefully).

The last scene of the Act, the scene of Violaine's departure, is introduced by the following note: 'Diese ganze Szene ironisch; alle lügen. sie sehn sich nicht in die Augen.' (This whole scene ironically; they are all lying; they avoid each other's eyes.) As for the scene of the miracle in Act III, it has been particularly well worked over; there is scarcely a reply which does not have its marginal note, often indicating also the gestures and the movements of the two sisters. It is in this scene, too, that there occasionally appears someone's handwriting which is certainly not Hegner's, but which one cannot with any certainty identify as Claudel's. Nevertheless it is an extremely Claudelian remark that one can make out scrawled above the words of Violaine replying to the desperate cry of Mara – 'Violaine, je suis une infortunée, et ma douleur est plus grande que la tienne!' 'Plus grande, soeur?': 'Von überirdischer Ironie' (With heavenly irony).

But Claudel was not content with crossing out the text. Here and there in the margin we find large signs in red crayon, vigorously drawn. They are of four different kinds, and Hegner has carefully reproduced them on the fly-leaf, with their meanings. The long cross upside down means, he says, a crescendo ⊥. The same long cross, the right way up, a decrescendo †. A circle with a vertical stroke through it means the culminating point of a role φ. Finally, a double cross means 'die musikalisch gleitenden Stellen' (passages of musical flow) ‡. According to these indications Pierre de Craon reaches his culminating point in the line in the Prologue: 'Il est dur d'être lépreux . . .' and in the following line, both being marked with a crossed circle. Violaine has her crossed circle at the moment of communicating her great secret (p. 87) and two pages later, Jacques Hury has his with the words that have already been quoted: 'Infâme, réprouvée!' In the scene of the miracle, there is another culminating point at Violaine's words: 'Tu me donnes bien son corps! donne le reste à Dieu', and at Mara's words: 'Est-ce que j'ai cinquante enfants à m'arracher du corps?' (p. 126); and immediately before the silence in which the bells of Christmas are going to ring forth, Claudel has marked with his red circle Violaine's tortured line: 'Pourquoi ne me laisses-tu en paix? pourquoi viens-tu ainsi me tourmenter dans ma tombe?'

The two single crosses have only been used once in the Prologue, for Pierre de Craon (p. 11). Of the two questions which form three lines, the first is a crescendo 'N'avais-je pas assez de pierres à assembler . . .', the second a decrescendo. The double crosses, that is to say the musical passages, are much more numerous: three in the prologue, all of them being part of Pierre de Craon's role (pp. 13, 17–18, 29), Jacques Hury's long passage in Act II: 'Violaine, quelles sont ces paroles étranges. . . .' (pp. 85–6), two of Mara's speeches in the miracle scene and the beginning of Mara's confession in the last Act, then the speeches of Pierre de Craon and Anne Vercors (pp. 170, 175 and 178). Moreover Hegner, at the beginning of the last scene of the play, noted: 'Von jetzt ab gleitet alles musikalisch hin' (From now on everything glides along musically) which echoes what Claudel wrote to Marie Kalff before the performance of *L'Annonce* in Paris: '. . . la dernière scène est toute de musique' and: 'l'opéra qu'est le final'[9]. And if there were any further need to point out the importance of music for the poet Claudel, the miracle scene would provide us with further proof. One finds the marginal instruction *Crescendo* four times (pp. 118, 121–2, 126, 129) and from page to page there are continual musical notations: *ff* together with a crossed circle in pencil (p. 122), *Cantilene* (p. 123), *sforzato* (p. 124) and *Kadenz* (p. 125), the three last being probably in Claudel's writing.

The two double crosses in the miracle scene need a commentary: they have been vigorously crossed out in pencil, and each replaced by a note. 'Je n'ai pas livré mon corps', says Violaine, and her sister replies: 'Douce Violaine! menteuse Violaine . . .' Only a poet who was working on the principle of 'De la musique avant toute chose' could describe this passage as musical, and the note *sehr ironisch* (very ironically) is certainly more suitable to it (p. 120). The same is true of p. 129 where the musical crosses had referred to Mara's despairing line: 'Rends-moi cet enfant que je t'ai donné...' and where it has been replaced by the word *schreiend* (screaming) written by Hegner.

At what moment did the rounded writing of Wolf Dohrn (?) begin in its turn to operate in the margins of the *Regiebuch*? Almost certainly when the work of Claudel and Hegner was already fairly advanced. We find it in the *sehr ironisch* above the cancelled cross, a fact which proves that Claudel and Dohrn collaborated very closely. It was he who gave the character of the mother before her entry on the stage at the beginning of Act I: DIE MUTTER: Spiel am Anfang nuanciert, belebt, veränderlich, sagt nie offen was sie denkt, nachher traurig und nachdenklich.' (THE MOTHER: should be played at the beginning with a certain amount of nuance, lively, variable, never says openly what she is thinking; later, sorrowful and thoughtful) (p. 34). He placed innumerable NBs in the margin to attract attention. But above all he did his job as producer and marked the entrances and exits of the characters, and their place on the stage.

It is at this point that we must remember the effect of *Orfeo* on Claudel. It is through Dohrn[10] that we know that he wanted to adopt Jaques-Dalcroze's 'décor stylisé au maximum'[11] for his play. Only three of the long scenic directions in *L'Annonce* have been entirely crossed out: the description of the kitchen at Combernon (Act I), that of the fountain of l'Adoue (II, iii) and that of Géyn (III, ii). But it is obvious from the producer's instructions that the play was performed on the three planes mentioned by Darius Milhaud, and one often reads notes such as the following, which comes at the beginning of the first Act: 'Erste Bühne' (first Stage); or this other one, at the end of the following scene: 'Mutter geht die Treppe links... hinauf zur 2. Bühne and links ab...' (the mother goes up the steps on the left to the second stage, and then off left) (p. 53). The appearance of Violaine 'encadrée par une sorte d'ogive lumineuse', which Milhaud mentioned, and which seems in doubtful taste to us nowadays, was part of A. de Salzmann's design for Act IV.[12] But nothing in the *Regiebuch* indicates this or gives us any ground for supposition.

★

Without taking account of the importance of the performance of *L'Annonce faite à Marie* at Hellerau in the history of Claudel's works in Germany,[13] and limiting ourselves to the influence of these performances on Claudel himself, it is worth noting that more than thirty years later, when the old poet produced his 'version pour la scène' for the new production of *l'Annonce* at the Théâtre Hébertot, he certainly seems to have remembered his work with Jakob Hegner. Thus, of the twelve cuts made in the Prologue of *Verkündigung*, five are the same as those in the 'forme définitive' of 1948, which begins in exactly the same way as the text in the *Regiebuch*. And we have other evidence that Hellerau made a lasting impression on Claudel. In his 'Essai de mise en scène et notes diverses' for *Les Choéphores*, he was to say: 'J'imagine de préférence pour la représentation des *Choéphores* une scène faite d'éléments mobiles, comme celle de Hellerau, en Saxe.' [14] And again, in connection with *Les Euménides*: 'J'aurais voulu établir ici une mise en scène pour les *Euménides* comme je l'ai fait pour les *Choéphores* mais les idées que j'ai à ce sujet, appropriées soit au théâtre d'Orange soit à celui de Hellerau, ne sont pas encore au point.' [15] These notes were written in 1920. On 10 December 1942, at Brangues, Claudel completed his Essay *Sur la musique*, addressed to Arthur Honegger. In it he speaks of a conception of music entirely based on rhythm, on time, and continues: 'C'est pourquoi je dois avouer que j'ai la plus grande sympathie pour les idées de Jaques-Dalcroze. J'ai assisté autrefois, à Hellerau, a une représentation de l'*Orphée* de Gluck, réglée par lui, que j'ai trouvée de toute beauté.' [16]

Thus, thirty years later, the poet still speaks in the same way as in his 1913 letter to the *NRF* which finished thus: 'Les représentations de l'*Orphée* de Gluck à Hellerau ont été incomparables. C'est la première fois, depuis les jours de la Grèce, que l'on voit de la véritable beauté au théâtre.'[17]

But the fact that Claudel remembered Hellerau when meditating on two of his favourite themes, Aeschylus and music, proves nothing with regard to *L'Annonce*, in which, moreover, music seems to have played only a small role, except for the obligatory bells (II, iv and III, iii). The *Regiebuch* only once gives the marginal instruction 'Musik' at the moment when Violaine, with the dead child in her arms, says to her sister: 'Son âme vit en Dieu. Elle suit l'Agneau. . . '; this is therefore just before the moment which Claudel designated as the culminating point of the roles of Violaine and Mara in the resurrection scene.

Did the performance of October 1913 exercise a specific influence on Claudel the dramatist, or at least on the author of *L'Annonce faite à Marie*? It would be difficult to say. It is true that in his correspondence with Lugné Poe Claudel does his utmost to make the director of the Théâtre de l'Oeuvre share his enthusiasm for Hellerau – in vain, which is hardly surprising.[18] In 1912, Lugné Poe had entrusted the production of *L'Annonce* – in which he himself was to play the role of Anne Vercors – to Jean Variot, who had just spent two years in Munich studying with Julius Klein the new system of doing without scenery; here is an example of it:

Il n'y avait rien, absolument rien que du noir opaque autour de Violaine et de Mara dans la scène sublime de la résurrection de l'enfant. Mais un rayon rougeâtre envoyé par un projecteur déplorable venait frapper les deux femmes assises. A Munich, nous savions ce que valait ce *truc* simplet. Chose à peine croyable, le public parisien de la générale a applaudi ce décor qui n'existait pas.[19]

Of course there is lack of scenery and lack of scenery, and Hellerau was nothing like Munich, as 'Wolf Dohrn tries to make us understand in his article on Claudel in the *Claudel-Programmbuch*.[20] But can one expect the French to make the distinction? In the article he wrote in 1955, at the death of Claudel, Jean Variot does not mention Hellerau . . . What is certain is that the absence of scenery in the production at the Théâtre de l'Oeuvre had not brought about a conversion in Claudel to the new German system. Jean Variot tells us that the poet of *L'Annonce* was very keen to show his native Tardenois, and above all the black caves of Géyn to his Parisian producer. In 1955, for the revival of

45

L'Annonce, the Comédie Française was to create the realistic scenery described in the text – the same which the poet had so blithely sacrificed in 1913 at Hellerau – and Jean Variot assures us 'que rien n'a été fait au Théâtre Français sans son assentiment formel'.[21] One may well ask oneself what is the worth of the formal assent of a man of well over eighty, completely deaf, but still appreciative of success; and one can recall that even in 1912, with regard to the modifications which Lugné Poe wanted to make to his play, Claudel wrote to Marie Kalff that he let himself be persuaded far too easily.[22] Why should he have tried to revive on that French stage which had traditionally remained the most opposed to any new system, the Hellerau experiment, which had already been dead for thirty-five years? At all events, I leave the problem of explaining the contradiction, if contradiction there be, to the Claudelians.

NOTES

1. *NRF*, II (1913), 309.
2. Paul Claudel, 'Wolf Dohrn', *NRF*, I (1914), 498.
3. *NRF*, II (1913), 475.
4. ibid., II, 822.
5. *Paul Claudel et André Gide. Correspondance, 1899-1926*, Paris: Gallimard, 1949, p. 211.
6. In 1923 Jakob Hegner gave his precious copy to Dr Egon Wellesz who has allowed me, with his customary generosity, to use it for the present article. I would like to express my thanks to him here.
7. Dr E. M. Landau's translation is much closer to Claudel's original.
8. *Jacques Rivière et Paul Claudel. Correspondance, 1907-14*, Paris: Plon, 1926, p. 186.
9. 'Lettres de Paul Claudel à Marie Kalff', *La Table Ronde* (avril 1955), pp. 70, 73.
10. Wolf Dohrn, *Claudels Verkündigung in Hellerau, Das Claudel-Programm-Buch*, Hellerauer Verlag, 1913, p. 83.
11. The phrase is Darius Milhaud's, art. cit., *NRF*, II (1913), 821.
12. See 'Claudel homme de théâtre. Correspondance avec Lugné-Poe', *Cahiers Paul Claudel 5*, NRF (1964), p. 129; and *Comoedia*, 4.10.1913.
13. cf. Margret Andersen, *Claudel et l'Allemagne*, Cahier canadien Claudel 3, ed. de L'Université d'Ottawa, 1965. (A work from which I have obtained a great deal of information.)

14. *Théâtre I*, Pl., Paris, 1947, p. 996.
15. ibid., p. 1003.
16. *Oeuvres en prose*, Pl., Paris, 1965, p. 156.
17. *NRF*, II (1913), 476.
18. 'Claudel homme de théâtre. Correspondance avec Lugné-Poe', op. cit., pp. 117–32.
19. Jean Variot, 'L'Annonce faite à Marie au Théâtre de l'Oeuvre en 1912', *La Table Ronde* (avril 1955), p. 64.
20. art. cit., p. 83.
21. art. cit., p. 65.
22. 'Lettres de Paul Claudel à Marie Kalff', *La Table Ronde* (avril 1955), p. 70: 'Je suis loin d'être aussi intransigeant qu'on se l'imagine, et ne suis au contraire, par goût naturel, que trop enclin aux tripatouillages.'

4 · Providence's play: *Le Soulier de satin*

MICHAEL WOOD

Je devins un opéra fabuleux—Arthur Rimbaud

THERE IS A CURIOUS, frequently forgotten sequence in the Fourth Day of *Le Soulier de satin*. It concerns the sinking of the Armada and forms a distinct, although perhaps not immediately obvious, play within the play.[1]

The King of Spain – the second to appear in the play – is seen gazing into a skull of Aztec crystal. It shows the destruction of the Armada sent against England, and the floating corpse of the Spanish admiral, the handsome Duke of Medina Sidonia. The King has barely finished consoling himself with the thought that he never really hoped to win, when his Chamberlain enters, jubilant with the news of victory. One shadow: the Duke of Medina Sidonia is drowned. Theatrical entry of the Actress. On her knees before the King, she begs that her lover, Felipe de Medina Sidonia, may not be sent to govern England. She fears that Mary Stuart may offer him her hand, and make him King. But Mary Stuart, says the King, is not in England at the moment, she is at his feet. The Actress has but to play the part of Mary Stuart to win back her Felipe – rather, to win back all that answers to the name of Felipe. She is to play the part in the presence of Don Rodrigue. As Mary Stuart, escaped to Spain, she is to persuade him to ask for the throne of England. This is the man the King requires: Don Rodrigue, sometime Viceroy of the Indies, General in Japan, at present one-legged purveyor of holy images, living on a broken-down boat. He has but to ask for England to receive it.

The Actress prepares. Her dressing-room is represented by a toilet table and large mirror attached to the drop curtain by clearly visible strings. Such a wonderful part, the best she has ever played. If only you're as lovely as you was the other night, ma'am, says her dresser . . . Whereupon the curtain rises, taking with it table, mirror and all. The Actress is on the wrong side of the curtain. Another actress has taken her part, another actress is playing Mary Stuart on Rodrigue's boat. She plays well. She gains Rodrigue's confidence, although he does not commit himself. He will go to England if he wishes. One feels he will wish.

The court. By now everyone – except Rodrigue – knows of the disaster of the Armada. But none of the arrangements has been changed, the audience the King has granted to Rodrigue will still take place. The courtiers have been instructed to show all deference, as to one who is to be made King of England. Rodrigue appears. The King greets him. Rodrigue is questioned by the King and various ministers as to his plans, his hopes, his resources. His condition that the Americas be left open to the conquered country provokes consternation, and the mockery reaches its height. Is there anyone but Rodrigue to govern England? No, cry all. King and court have been sufficiently amused. Rodrigue is dismissed. The charade is over.

Three acts, perfectly self-contained. One thinks of an Old Testament story of God trying His servant, or of the master in the parable reaping where he has not sown. For what is curious about the King's fabrication is its gratuitousness. The King has certain reasons for his action, of course:

> Dieu se moque du Roi d'Espagne. Pourquoi le Roi d'Espagne ne se moquerait-il pas de Don Rodrigue? C'est dit! Il le fera souverain de ce royaume là-bas, dont l'espérance pour lui, il l'a vu, vient de s'engloutir dans les flots.[2]

This is the explanation in the stage version. It is true that Rodrigue and his wreck of a ship have for some time been a floating affront to the King:

Quelle est cette insolence inouïe de promener ainsi sous les yeux du Roi en ce moment même où il tient ses assises solennelles sur la mer,

Cette espèce de détritus et de guenille qu'est devenu l'homme que jadis il avait chargé de représenter dans l'autre monde Sa propre et personnelle Majesté? (p. 861)

The King has here a chance of fitting revenge. It may also be a sound political move: finding a scapegoat to turn the sense of failure at the defeat of the Armada into general laughter, into that sense of superiority which comes with mockery. But such reasons are not more than an impetus. There remains the elaborate execution, the gratuitous invention, the structure of the fabrication. The King offers Rodrigue a country which is not his to offer. He promises to return to the Actress a man who is dead. He involves his whole court in a cruel masquerade. What are we to make of this?

First, we must remember that *Le Soulier de satin* is much concerned with *creation*, in both senses of the word: with the divine or poetic act and with the created world, the work of the six days.

'La scène de ce drame est le monde . . .' (p. 651)

'C'est moi qui ai tout à créer,' says the Actress, 'les paroles et la musique . . .' (p. 886)

We must remember what the term *to create* means, in Claudel's definition, 'ce que signifie le terme *créer*, c'est à-dire faire de rien'.[3] And we must remember that for Claudel the created world was a *work of art*,

. . . que la création après tout est une oeuvre, que toute oeuvre obéit à une raison qui est sa raison d'être, qu'elle a une logique intime, qu'elle est soumise à certaines conditions extérieures *données*, qu'elle prête l'oreille à des lois que ne sont pas ces lois de compétence courte et subordonnée qu'on appelle lois scientifiques et administratives, mais ces lois vraiment créatrices que tout artiste porte au fond de lui-même, bien qu'il n'ait ni le gôut ni le talent de les formuler, et qu'on appelle *lois de composition*.[4]

The puzzle begins to clear. The King is an artist. He has created a *work* in exactly the sense defined above, and created it from nothing. His curious comedy echoes the improbable, playful artistry of the labours of God.[5] More than that. Since the King is not only playful but cruel, he is a *parody* picture of God and of the artist. He is the artist as the eyes of science and administration see him. He is the divine Artist as He appears to the mind of rational man.

This view of the King is reinforced by the repeated suggestion that to turn one's back on His Very Catholic Majesty is to turn away from God. This is the double treason of Don Camille, and the arrogance of Rodrigue:

Il y a trop longtemps qu'il fuit jusqu'aux extrémités de la terre Notre présence, se vantant de faire où Nous n'étions pas, Notre oeuvre et de gagner pour Nous la longeur de son ombre par les moyens que lui-même a inventés et combinés. (p. 878)

The King's words here correspond to the prayer of Rodrigue's dying brother, the Jesuit priest:

. . . et maintenant sans doute parce qu'il a quitté Votre noviciat il se figure qu'il Vous tourne le dos,

Son affaire à ce qu'il imagine n'étant pas d'attendre mais de conquérir et de posséder

Ce qu'il peut, comme s'il y avait rien qui ne Vous appartînt et comme s'il pouvait être ailleurs que là où Vous êtes. (p. 654)

The King and his scenario, then, are an image of God and His inscrutable purposes. They are thus an expression in brief and in caricature of what *Le Soulier de satin* is at length and with less distortion: a picture of God at work. The play is experimental philosophy. The author has built '. . . une espèce d'univers réduit, où ses essais dans un milieu artificiellement simplifié et rétréci ont une espèce de valeur expérimentale'. [6] Its heroes are test-figures in a test-case, put in a situation, not to show the answer already arrived at, but to generate an answer as they act. Hence the insistence, throughout *Le Soulier de satin*, on improvisation. The King and his little play stand in much the same relationship to the work as a whole as the episode of Diégo Rodriguez and Dona Austrégésile (pp. 894–8) stands to the story of Rodrigue and Prouhèze. They are at once a summary, an echo and a travesty. But with this difference: one of the characters here is the author himself. That is, the Author of the world which is the scene of the play; and the author of the play which is a reduction of that world. The summary is a reduction of the reduction.

There are similar projections of the author into the text to be found elsewhere in the play, similar reminders of the total image: the play as God in action. But where the King is perhaps more God than artist, or God as artist, the Irrepressible of the Second Day is chiefly the artist. Indeed, he is very much this particular artist. Claudel writes to a friend:

> Mon esprit se met par moments à ne plus procéder que par bonds soudains et disparitions instantanées. C'est au lecteur à se débrouiller avec ce lapin éperdu qui se cogne à tout les meubles, qu'il tâche moyen au bon moment de l'attraper par la patte ou par les oreilles, avant qu'il réintègre le chapeau du prestidigitateur! Ou si vous voulez, quand je frappe dans mes mains, je ne sais quels acteurs à demi-accoutrés tous à la fois vont répondre à mon appel pour prendre leur place dans la pièce improvisée dont je suis le désemparé régisseur.[7]

The Irrepressible does not clap his hands, but the figures he wishes to conjure appear too soon:

> ...je vous présente la maman de Don Rodrigue. (Entre Dona Honoria)
> L'IRRÉPRESSIBLE, *rugissant* – Restez où vous êtes! attendez que j'aille vous chercher,
> Sacrebleu! qui vous a dit de venir? Sortez! Sortez! (p. 717)

As he says:

52

C'est vexant, ce qui m'arrive. C'est pour cela que je n'ai pas
pu être peintre. Mes personnages commençaient à exister tout
à coup avant que je leur aie fendu l'oeil . . .

Quand je fais un chien, je n'ai pas achevé le derrière qu'il
commence à remuer la queue et qu'il se sauve sur trois pattes
sans attendre la tête. (p. 717)

And as Claudel wrote to Jammes: 'Vous savez très bien qu'un
écrivain n'est en somme que le témoin, souvent stupéfait, de son
oeuvre . . .' [8] The Irrepressible is a projection into the play of the
author confronted with the independent existence of his work,
with the unpredictable movements of his mind, the hoppings of
the rabbit. Yet he is at the same time the rabbit itself, and one of
the half-clad actors – 'J'aurais dû attendre mon costume' (p. 716).
He is at once the writer and his imagination, so often held in
check:

On se défie de mon ardeur, je mène les choses trop vite, en
deux foulées nous serions au but et le public serait trop content!
(p. 716)

He is the summary, the delegate of all the uncreated figures of
the author's mind:

C'est pourquoi l'auteur me tient en réserve, un en-cas si je
puis dire, avec tout un peuple de figurants qui font un grand
bruit de pieds dans les greniers de son imagination et dont vous
ne verrez jamais la figure. (p. 716)

He is also the bewildered producer:

Attention là-haut! Descendez les bandes d'air! la herse
sur résistance, le projecteur d'avant-scène côté jardin. (p. 717)

That many reviewers of performances of *Le Soulier de satin* –
both in 1943 and since – should assume this character of the
Irrepressible, amalgamated for the stage with that of the Announcer, to be a utility-measure, a device, is excusable, for in the stage-
version he does appear, in the Second Part and Epilogue, for this

purpose:[9] to explain scenes which would, had there been time, have been played. But here, in the original version, he explains nothing. He tells us that Rodrigue is sick at the home of his mother; that Prouhèze has arrived, but has not seen Rodrigue. Most of this we knew from the scene in the First Day between the Chinaman and the Negress (pp. 696–700); the rest we learn in the ensuing dialogue between Dona Honoria and Don Pélage (pp. 720–1). The Irrepressible makes no contribution to the exposition of a situation. If he has a function in the play at all, it is not as a narrator.

The same is true of the Announcer, who introduces the play. But where with the Irrepressible there was a suggestion of creation in the moment, of a magician producing things out of thin air –

> *Il sort et rentre avec Dona Prouhèze dont la main est posée sur son poing, avec l'air d'un magnétiseur qui amène son numéro . . .* (p. 718)

– the Announcer, although in a sense conjuring the play (does he not carry a wand?) is far more a showman than a magician, far more concerned with introducing a spectacle than creating figures. He is the crier of the 'grande foire':[10]

> Fixons, je vous prie, mes frères, les yeux sur ce point de l'Océan Atlantique . . . (p. 652)

And he describes the decorative curtain with its shipwreck and corpses and its heap of dead nuns. He describes it in detail. Again, this is dramatically unnecessary; we can see perfectly well what the curtain represents, and the following speech of the Jesuit priest is the real exposition. Like all showmen, the Announcer is not afraid to duplicate information. He has to sell his wares.

This is the rub. Showman, magician, artist, God, whatever these figures suggest, all insist on attention to their wares; to the work, the show. They join the spectators; stand back and see that it is good. And this particular show, to be good, must remain honestly, blatantly, obstinately a show. For the total image of the world and men in it as a play written and directed by God is dependent on the transparency of the play by Paul Claudel, It must be clearly a play, really a play, before it can be a play-image. It must admit its artificiality:

> *Les machinistes feront quelques aménagements nécessaires sous les yeux mêmes du public pendant que l'action suit son cours . . . Les indications de scène, quand on y pensera et que cela ne gênera pas le mouvement, seront ou bien affichées ou lues par le régisseur ou les acteurs eux-mêmes quitireront de leur poche ou se passeront de l'un à l'autre les papiers nécessaires.* (p. 649)

This is not just a joke in a preface. It is a serious suggestion for the staging of the play. This has been much misunderstood. Our great writer will have his fun, has been the feeling. But such stage-directions propose a whole style of production, and while easily forgotten by the literary reader of the play, or by someone who has seen Jean-Louis Barrault's sumptuous and perhaps over-solemn *mise-en-scène*, they must invade the play for anyone who gives it an adequate mental performance. The play is a spectacle, and the audience is never to be allowed to forget this:

> *Un bout de corde qui pend, une toile de fond mal tirée et laissant apparaître un mur blanc devant lequel passe et repasse le personnel sera du meilleur effet.* (p. 649)

> *Je suppose que ma pièce soit jouée par example un jour de Mardi-Gras à quatre heures de l'après-midi. Je rêve une grande salle chauffée par un spectacle précédent, que le public envahit et que remplissent les conversations.* (p. 649)

The idea of the Mardi-Gras performance is that the public – 'le public n'a à voir que son plaisir' [11] – may consent to the spectacle for what it is, as they consent to a concert,[12] that they may know and enjoy their day off. Not, as has been suggested,[13] that the public may, in a moment of festivity, be taken off its guard and bombarded with the Truth. Gide excepted Claudel from his collection of Catholics who used the crucifix as a bludgeon.[14]

The audience is not attacked by *Le Soulier de satin* but it *is* more and more involved. Drama demands a theatre; players and public, not merely a stage. The three-planks-and-a-passion theory ignores this. 'Il y a la scène et la salle,'[15] says Claudel in 1894. Later he is concerned to abolish this very distinction. In the Noh, public and players are one: '. . . il n'y a pas un drame et un public face à face correspondant de chaque côté d'une fissure de fiction et de feu. Ils entrent l'un dans l'autre.'[16]

The Noh was for Claudel 'une véritable école professionnelle du dramaturge'.[17] *L'Oiseau noir dans le soleil levant* was published only two years after *Le Soulier de satin*, which was written for the most part in Tokyo.

There is an invitation to complicity in so many movements of the play. This would seem to be the function of the Announcer and the Irrepressible: to serve as a linkage, a *truchement*, between the characters and the audience, to involve us in the fake, literally to 'let us in on' the spectacle.

> Nous ne sommes plus à Cadix, nous sommes dans la Sierra Quelquechose, au milieu d'une de ces belles forêts qui ont fait la célébrité de la Catalogne.
> Un pic, c'est là qu'est le château de Don Rodrigue; Don Rodrigue est ici, fort mal en point, sa blessure le chatouille, je crois bien qu'il va crever . . . je me trompe, il guérira ou la pièce serait finie . . . (pp. 716-7)

> La maman de Don Rodrigue, Dona Quelquechose . . . Honoria vous va-t-il? (p. 717)

If we are asked thus to co-operate, it is made very easy for us. We are addressed as children – 'Ecoutez bien, ne toussez pas et essayez de comprendre un peu . . .' (p. 652) – but we are not to be the dupes of this fiction:

> . . . je vous demande la permission de vous amener Dona Prouhèze. Quel nom! comme ça lui donne un petit air vrais-emblable! (p. 717)

('Elle s'appelait un drôle de nom,' says a soldier, much later, 'quelque chose comme Ogresse ou Bougresse . . .') (p. 925).

The Irrepressible throws a piece of chalk with which he has been drawing into the auditorium (p. 717). This is a kind of pun on that weary phrase 'passer la rampe'. *Le Soulier de satin* gets over the footlights in spite of what appears to be a continual shattering of the illusion of Spain, a conquistador and his love, by the illusion of a *play* about Spain, a conquistador and his love. It adds a dimension. And this dimension includes us. We are spectators of this Spain and its hero, but accomplices in the play about them. Thus a curtain representing a shipwreck with a Jesuit priest tied to a mast is succeeded by a set showing a shipwreck with a Jesuit priest tied to a mast. The Announcer describes the priest:

> Le voici qui parle comme il suit: Seigneur, je vous remercie de m'avoir ainsi attaché ... Mais c'est lui qui va parler ...
> (p. 652)

The curtain rises and the priest speaks:

> Seigneur, je vous remercie de m'avoir ainsi attaché ...
> (p. 652).

This is a cinema-trick (in 1925), the family-photograph becoming the family.

We are not invited, as the Elizabethans were, to consider a plant-pot a forest; but to smile at all stage forests. The Elizabethan theatre demanded assent; this kind of set –

> *Un vieux bateau délabré et rapiécé qui fait voile péniblement vers le port. (Si c'est trop compliqué à représenter une simple bouteille dans la main de Diégo Rodriguez contenant un bateau à voiles fera l'affaire.)*
> (p. 894)

– requires collaboration. There is a knowing wink at the audience; both author and public *know*. No one is deceived; no illusions:

> *Il y aura, si l'on veut, au fond de la scène, un écran où l'on pourra projeter des scènes et peintures appropriées de manière que le public puisse passer le temps pendant que les acteurs racontent leurs petites histoires.* (p. 853)

The legendary Letter to Rodrigue belongs to this policy of baring the structure, showing the skeleton. This letter –

> . . . depuis dix ans la lettre passe ainsi de main à l'autre,
>   De Barcelone à Macao, d'Anvers à Naples,
>   Apportant à celui qui comme ressource dernière l'abat sur la table,
>   Le succès, du trépas incontinent suivi. (p. 785)

– is clearly not simply a means of bringing Rodrigue to Mogador. Claudel is not 'mocking his own failure to hit upon a more convincing device'. [18] There would be no difficulty at all in finding a more convincing device: Prouhèze would have only to write her letter later. The letter is an exact transcription of the mechanics of Providence: hindering where they are wrong, but not finally controverting, the actions of man's free will. Is this not Prouhèze's prayer, as she deposits her slipper with the Virgin? that she may *limp* towards evil? (p. 671). The letter, taking ten years to reach its destination, limps towards Rodrigue. But to reveal the working of Providence is to strip bare the framework of the play, which is Providence in action. The letter, the agent of the dramatic climax of the work, falls from a very spurious décor –

> . . . *cette rangée de fenêtres dans un plâtras agréablement rose ou bleu d'une maison de Gênes transportée pour les besoins de la couleur locale à Panama* (p. 792)

– and is picked up by a stage-hand. The strings could not be more visible.

The Announcer and the Irrepressible, then, do not represent isolated moments of mockery of the stage-convention, but are projections into the text itelf of something that is constant in the mode of presentation: an insistence on the fake, an invitation to complicity. In the last Two Days, this role of linkage between stage and auditorium is taken over by the orchestra. This is also an oriental technique:

L'orchestre . . . a moins le rôle musical qu'il ne sert de support à tout, jouant, pour ainsi dire, le souffleur et répondant pour le public.[19]

We are represented in attention by music:

. . . n'y aurait-il pas deux musiques, l'une active et l'autre passive, l'une qui est voix, et l'autre qui est oreille, une musique qui écoute?[20]

In the tired heat of Panama (pp. 812–18) we, the listeners, are duplicated, behind the set, by a listening orchestra. Its intermitten attention – it accompanies Isabel, then stops; it supports her, then contradicts – represents us perhaps unfairly. It represents some of us very well. The orchestra in the wall is an echoing-board, throwing back in sound our wavering sympathy. In the floating court of the King of Spain, the orchestra anticipates both our boredom and our ironic comment.

L'orchestre se désinteresse de tout ce qui va suivre et s'occupe pour se désennuyer à imiter les plongeons et ascensions de la mer et les sentiments des gens qui ont mal au coeur. (p. 910)

It will occasionally support the establishment –

. . . *murmure de réprobation dans l'assistance auquel l'orchestre s'associe après avoir pris le temps de la réflexion* (p. 918)

– but let a minister get a little pompous, and it will return to its sickly mimicry (p. 918).

But it was not the music which prompted Gabriel Marcel to say 'Il me semble que j'exprimerais assez exactement ma pensée en disant qu'à mes yeux *Le Soulier de satin* correspond au moment infiniment dangereux où l'œuvre claudélienne toute entière passe sur le plan de l'*opéra*'.[21] The play moves on to the level of opera because it is so frankly a spectacle. The danger of the moment is for drama; springing from the interposition of the Play – in *Christophe Colomb* and *Jeanne au bûcher* it will be the Book – between fiction and public. By the thickening of the artifact, the impact is weakened. Claudel himself sees a distinction between drama and spectacle: 'Comprenez qu'une pièce de Double Véesse c'est un spectacle qu'on vous sert à regarder. Ce n'est pas un drame, c'est des évènements à la file qu'on vous invite à regarder'.[22] This is not true for Shakespeare, but it is true for *Le Soulier de satin*; and the play is coherent at this level. A lessening of drama is not necessarily a loss to the theatre. There is no illusion broken by the insistent Play, or Book, for there is never really an illusion to break. We never fully suspend disbelief, remit the judgment that we are not seeing a forest[23] – we often discuss productions, *compare* forests, all of them visibly false. The operative word is conviction – 'cette force mystérieuse qu'on appelle la conviction'[24] – and this is based on the consistency, the coherence of the work at the level chosen, whether fourth-wall drama or opera; a kind of fidelity to a set of self-imposed conditions.

At the level of spectacle, of the play, *Le Soulier de satin* is perfectly coherent and consistent. It is faithful to the two fundamentals which govern it. First to the reversible image of the artist as God and God as an artist; of the play as a world and human action as a play – '. . . nous sommes comme les acteurs d'un drame très intéressant écrit par un auteur infiniment sage et bon où nous tenons un rôle essentiel, mais où il nous est impossible de connaître d'avance la moindre péripétie.'[25] But there is no question of the world being a stage; the metaphor is concerned with the *theatre* as a unit, with players and public. This is the second fundamental; that the play, God's and Claudel's, is a *play*, an entertainment. The public, who assent to music as music (what else could it be?), must assent to this theatre as theatre. They shall have no choice. This is the honest fake, the thick-stringed marionette – which is perhaps the meaning of that curious scene where the Actress finds herself on the wrong side of the curtain. There is too much preparation, she does not see the strings so clearly visible to everyone else. She takes herself seriously, mistakes a play for life (the reverse is true) and thus belongs to our side of the curtain, to the mass of real people living serious lives.

She is a professional, her art has become a business. The curtain goes up without her.

For the two fundamentals are not distinct. The spectacle is not a playful basis for an earnest metaphor. It is *as* play that the theatre is most valuable, it is *as* play that the metaphor comes nearest its reference. 'Ne voyez-vous pas le principe de tout un art éclatant et généreux dans ce chapitre des Proverbes, où l'on voit la Sagesse "jouant" sur l'abîme dans une liberté sublime?' [26] Claudel asked this question of Gide. As Stanislas Fumet has said, 'Claudel est un grand homme qui ne se prend pas au sérieux: il n'en dit que mieux les choses éternelles.' [27]

NOTES

1. *Le Soulier de satin*, version intégrale, in Paul Claudel, *Théâtre* II, Pl., Paris 1956, pp. 869–79, 885–94, 908–19. Further references to the complete version of *Le Soulier de satin* are to this edition and are taken up into the text. Unless otherwise indicated, works and remarks identified in these notes are by Claudel.

2. *Le Soulier de satin*, édition pour la scène, Paris: Gallimard, 1944, pp. 220–1.

3. *Figures et paraboles*, Paris: Gallimard, 1936, p. 152.

4. ibid., pp. 134–5.

5. cf. ibid, pp. 147–8. 'Mais ce qu'il y a de plus profond dans la nature, c'est l'humour, l'espièglerie . . .'

6. 'Introduction à quelques oeuvres', *Les Cahiers des amis des livres*, 1er cahier, Paris: La Société des amis des livres, 1920, p. 17.

7. *Positions et propositions II*, Paris: Gallimard, 1934, pp. 151–2.

8. *Paul Claudel, Francis Jammes, Gabriel Frizeau. Correspondance, 1897–1938*, Paris: Gallimard, 1952, p. 62.

9. *Le Soulier de satin*, édition pour la scène, pp. 161–5, 219–23.

10. The phrase is that of Georges Perros, writing in the *NRF*, 33 (1.9.1955), 494.

11. Interview with Frédéric Lefèvre in *Les Nouvelles littéraires*, 18.4.1925.

12. cf. ibid. 'On accepte pour la musique ce qu'on n'accepte pas pour la poésie. Quel dommage que les spectateurs n'accordent pas à une oeuvre poétique la même patience, la même bonne volonté qu'ils apportent à l'audition d'une symphonie, d'un concerto.'

13. By Louis Barjon, in *Paul Claudel*, Paris: Editions universitaires, 1953, p. 63; and by Wallace Fowlie, in *Paul Claudel*, London: Bowes & Bowes, 1957, p. 71.

14. *Paul Claudel et André Gide. Correspondance 1899–1926*, Paris: Gallimard, 1949, p. 189.

15. *L'Echange*, 1ère version, *Théâtre I*, Pl., Paris, 1956, p. 676.
16. *L'Oiseau noir dans le soleil levant*, Paris: Gallimard, 1929, p. 90.
17. 'Le Drame et la musique', *Le Livre de Christophe Colomb*, Paris: Gallimard, 1935, p. 21.
18. The suggestion is that of Ernest Beaumont, in *The Theme of Beatrice in the plays of Claudel*, London: Rockliff, 1954, p. 71.
19. *Connaissance de l'Est*, *Oeuvre poétique*, Pl., Paris, 1957, p. 40.
20. *Figures et paraboles*, p. 164.
21. *Les Nouvelles littéraires*, 21.4.1949.
22. *Conversation sur Jean Racine*, Paris: Gallimard, 1955, p. 11.
23. cf. S. T. Coleridge, *Literary Remains II*, London: William Pickering, 1836, p. 38.
24. 'Le Drame et la musique', loc. cit., p. 15.
25. *Positions et propositions, II*, pp. 18–19.
26. *Paul Claudel et André Gide. Correspondance 1899–1926*, p. 52.
27. *La Vie intellectuelle*, 10.7.1935.

5 · *Jeanne d'Arc au bûcher* and its place in the work of Claudel

MOYA LAVERTY

JEANNE D'ARC AU BÛCHER has generally either been overlooked by critics or summarily dismissed as an extravaganza, operatic and clownish at the same time, in which Claudel vented his spleen upon the judges of Rouen. Slight as the work is, however, it merits a more careful and sympathetic assessment and its real importance will, I hope, emerge from a closer consideration of the text itself, of its relationship to some of the other plays, and of Claudel's concept of the figure of Jeanne d'Arc.

Jeanne d'Arc au bûcher is not an historical drama like Péguy's *Jeanne d'Arc*, not a 'chronicle play' like Shaw's *Saint Joan*, nor yet an opera like that of Jules Barbier set to music by Gounod. It is, as the sub-title *Oratorio dramatique* implies, a dramatic poem set to music. It is unfair to the work to take only the text into consideration, for Claudel's text and Honegger's music are interdependent, together creating atmosphere and symbol, a fact which Claudel himself considered to be of the first importance:

> Pour représenter, pour rendre une fois de plus intelligibles au public moderne cette Passion et cette ascension de Jeanne d'Arc, il m'a semblé que la parole ne suffisait pas. Il fallait pour la porter, pour la supporter, pour l'emporter, un élément ample et lyrique. C'est la voix, ce sont *les voix* sous l'histoire et sous l'action qu'il s'agissait de faire entendre, et c'est pourquoi il était indispensable d'avoir recours à la musique. C'est elle qui crée l'atmosphère, c'est elle qui entre la scène et la salle établit une ambiance commune, c'est elle qui intensifie le rythme, c'est elle qui propose à toutes les passions l'ouverture de l'accord et du chœur, c'est elle qui imprègne de sentiment et de pensée la parole, et en même temps qu'elle parle, c'est elle aussi qui écoute.[1]

63

In fact it was Honegger who suggested the subject, and Claudel's intention is to communicate emotion and perception through the combined resources of poetry and music. He uses the rhythms of music and speech, the values of harmonies and discords, images and symbols not in literary form alone, but also visual and aural. In the first scene of the *oratorio* there is no dialogue, no action, the stage is in total obscurity. This foreboding darkness is first pierced by the dismal howl of a dog, which is repeated as the orchestra adds a note which is 'half sob, half sinister laughter'. At the third cry the choir is introduced, only to lapse again shortly into silence. The ternary pattern is the fundamental rhythm which beats throughout the work. These three initial moments of the first scene are followed by two more phrases, each isolated by a short meditative silence. The desolation of the opening is replaced by the *Voix de la Nuit* mingling with an echo of Trimazô's song and the hint of a nightingale. In the final phrase the choir rises to a muffled crescendo, dying away again as the *Voix du Ciel* intone three times *Jeanne Jeanne Jeanne*. The whole movement of the oratorio from darkness to hope and finally to victory and apotheosis is thus foretold by the three motifs, the howling of the dog, Trimazô s song and the name of Jeanne thrice repeated by the heavenly voices.

The resources of orchestra, choir, lighting, leitmotive and the rhythms of speech and music are the mainstay of the work throughout. The ternary rhythms have incantatory force:

Jeanne	Jeanne	Jeanne
Hérétique	Sorcière	Relapse

Ennemie de Dieu – Ennemie du Roi – Ennemie du Peuple.
Qu'on l'enlève! – qu'on la tue! – qu'on la brûle!

(sc. iii, p. 1203)[2]

The choir constantly takes up these incantations and repeats them as a recurrent refrain, insistent in Latin as in French:

LA VOIX: Stryga!
LE CHOEUR: Pereat!
LA VOIX: Haeretica!

LE CHOEUR: Pereat!
LA VOIX: Relapsa!
LE CHOEUR: Pereat!

(sc. iii, p. 1204; sc. iv, pp. 1208–9)

The oratorio is brought to an end by the thrice repeated quotation from the gospel, announced by the heavenly voices and taken up by the voices on earth:

Personne n'a un plus grand amour que de donner sa vie pour ceux qu'il aime.

The structure of the work in itself follows the same ternary pattern. The three opening scenes of darkness and duologue between Jeanne and Frère Dominique are followed by three crowded and gaudy scenes recapitulating Jeanne's public life, the trial, the political background and Rheims, separated from each other by two brief moments of reflection, of renewed dialogue between the saint and her mentor; darkness finally yields to dawn and the voice of St Margaret chanting from above *Spira spera* introduces three scenes of meditation on the spiritual sense of Jeanne's vocation and death.

The underlying atmosphere is that of religious meditation, relieved contrapuntally by the contrasting style of the three scenes of Jeanne's public career. These do not re-enact events, but highlight their significance. The setting is not indicated by archaism of language or exactness of costume detail. 'Tout le drame se passe à la fin d'un Moyen Age de convention', Claudel might have written here as in the prologue to *L'Annonce*, thus capturing simultaneously the dual contexts of time and eternity. In Claudel's vision the trial emerges as a sinister farce, in which the members of the court wear sheep's heads, the judge is a pig (Cauchon: Cochon) and the clerk of the court an ass. The effect is nightmarish, like some fable of La Fontaine suddenly gone berserk and savage, while the burlesque Latin at times echoes the Vulgate and at times the *Malade Imaginaire*:

LE CHOEUR: Porcus! Porcus! Sit Porcus praeses noster. Non habemus alium judicem nisi Porcum. Vivat et à jamais vivat

Porcus porcorum! Dignus, dignus, dignus est praesidere in nostro praeclaro corpore!

(sc. iv, p. 1206)

The political background is outlined in the form of an allegory in which the historical protagonists appear as figures in a pack of cards. The King of France, the King of England, the Duke of Burgundy have as their respective queens Stupidity, Pride and Avarice, while Death and Licence are the fourth pair, representing the physical and moral disintegration resulting from war. The political game is not played out among these foreground figures but between the politicians and soldiers who appear as the jacks of the pack. They are the Duke of Bedford [sic] (Regent during the minority of Henry VI), the Duke of Luxemburg (captor of Jeanne and ally of the Burgundians), Guillaume de Flavy (captain of Compiègne, where Jeanne was captured; one tradition accuses him of betraying her, but the accusation is almost certainly false) and Regnault de Chartres (Archbishop of Rheims and diplomat; having opposed Jeanne's plans in the councils of Charles VII, he wrote a letter to the people of Rheims denouncing and disowning her as soon as she was captured). These events, political forces and motives are seen and presented not from the point of view of the historian, but of the moralist. Moreover Claudel chooses the traditions which give Jeanne's fate the greatest similarity to that of Christ: Flavy is a Judas-figure, Regnault de Chartres a kind of Caiaphas. This emphasis on even the externals of Jeanne's life as an *imitatio Christi* goes right back to the fifteenth century,[3] and was a parallel much underlined by Catholic writers of the nineteenth century eager for her canonization. The external resemblances to Christ's life serve to point out the inner fidelity to his example which is the essence of all Christian sanctity.

The two scenes of trial and politics are separated by a brief pause during which the dismal howl of a dog is heard once more. Frère Dominique now makes its significance clear by affirming:

C'est Yblis le désespéré qui hurle tout seul au fond de l'enfer!

The spirit of evil is thus perceived behind the human agents.

When the second of the two scenes ends the sinister cry is replaced by the hallowed sounds of church bells, at first tolling mournfully for one who is to die, but soon taking Jeanne back to her childhood as they begin to ring out joyfully and carry to her the voices of Saints Catherine and Margaret. The forces of evil have faded away and the way is opened for the outburst of rejoicing in the peasant carnival which celebrates the culmination of Jeanne's mission, the coronation of the Dauphin at Rheims. The dry dog-Latin of clerics and academics is replaced by the cheerful *patois* of Champagne. Two gigantic Gog and Magog-like figures symbolize the two halves of France, the wheat and the vine. Heurtebise is a windmill-giant with a straw hat and a millstone beneath his arm like a loaf; his accent is that of Picardy. His spouse, la Mère aux Tonneaux, represents the wine-regions and speaks with the accent of Burgundy. Their reunion is celebrated with merry-making and folksong as the unity of France is restored in the restoration of the rightful king. Unity replacing division, harmony discord, such is always Claudel's basic concept of salvation, earthly and eternal, and in the reunion of France he sees the human sense of Jeanne's mission. The problem of the sense of Jeanne d'Arc's vocation, for those who believe it to have been supernaturally inspired, is very great. Clearly it is necessary to look beyond the personal merits of Charles VII, who can be heavily criticized on many counts before and after Jeanne's coming. Claudel proposes the vaster concept of national unity. If he stopped short at such a point, he would have depicted a patriot, not a saint. Patriotism however has its dangers, as he was well aware.[4] God alone is man's end, and to put human being or nation in His place is to commit the sin of idolatry. Charles VII can no more be the reason why Jeanne was created than Rodrigue can be the ultimate goal of Prouhèze. The moment of triumph is the moment of danger for Jeanne, when Frère Dominique puts to her the crucial question:

Jeanne! Jeanne! Jeanne! Est-ce pour un Roi de chair que tu as donné ton sang virginal?

This question introduces the three final scenes which ponder the spiritual significance of Jeanne's life and death. The answer unfolds gradually as Jeanne contemplates the unfolding of spring in Normandy in this month of May in which she is to die and remembers the springtime in Lorraine, the perennial renewal of life and hope. To the heavenly voices calling 'Jeanne! Jeanne! Jeanne! Fille de Dieu, va! va! va!' is added a child's voice singing Trimazô's song, a folksong of joy and thanksgiving for the coming of May. Nature thus unfolds her message of hope and faith, with the joy and love which they inspire, all of which is symbolized in the bright sword which Jeanne accepts.

The final symbol of the work is that of flame, at once consuming and purifying, destroying and liberating. At the supreme moment of death, Frère Dominique fades away and the Blessed Virgin appears above the stake to which Jeanne is attached. In a movement of final exultation Jeanne bursts asunder the chains which bind her and accepts death with a cry of faith and love.

Claudel has written not a chronicle of Jeanne d'Arc but a meditation upon her life and death. The idea of a chronicle did not attract him, for he well realized the pitfalls which the historical subject presents, the limitations it imposes upon the artist's creative freedom, the false tone introduced only too often in any attempt to re-arrange the original. No play on Jeanne d'Arc is as moving as the documents of 1431 and 1456. Sentimentality and melodrama deform too frequently what in the original was simple, courageous and sincere. Claudel, therefore, did not at first welcome Honegger's suggestion, although he had written a poem dedicated to the saint in 1926.[5] She was certainly a figure who had permanently captured his interest and admiration. Louis Chaigne has printed a facsimile of a questionnaire which Claudel had once amused himself by completing; after the heading *Mes héroïnes dans l'histoire* he wrote the names of Jeanne d'Arc, Mary Stuart and Charlotte Corday, in that order.[6] None the less his enthusiasm for Honegger's suggestion was only born when, in a sudden inspiration, he conceived the idea of portraying not her career in itself, but uniquely the spiritual significance of

Jeanne's life and death. The idea came to him in the form of a symbol: Jeanne's hands in chains, lifted in a last sign of the cross at the moment of death, a sign of reconciliation and restoration of peace. 'La mission de Jeanne d'Arc . . . c'est avant tout une mission unificatrice. . . . Or, en ce Moyen Âge finissant, la France était divisée par le milieu entre Nord et Midi, comme la chrétienté l'était elle-même entre plusieurs papes.' [7]

Jeanne's mission has thus national and supra-national significance, the disorder of France being only an element of the wider divisions in Christendom. Nor is the meaning of her life and death limited to the healing of those divisions, for like all martyrdoms her death is a testimony, an act of faith valid for all times and for all peoples. To illuminate this aspect Claudel decided to isolate Jeanne from the context of her time and portray her only at the moment of death:

> Quant à Jeanne elle-meme, ce n'est pas la petite paysanne ni l'héroïne historique que j'ai essayé de représenter. C'est Sainte Jeanne parvenue à l'auréole. . . . On peut même imaginer que le souverain Père, avant de l'admettre en ce lieu où toutes les larmes sont essuyées, lui permet du haut du bûcher, et à la lumière, si je puis dire, de sa propre combustion, de relire page à page et comme à rebours toute l'histoire de sa vie, depuis Rouen jusqu'à Domrémy, et c'est dans la conscience pleinement réalisée de la mission qui lui était confiée que, dans un cri qui est une flamme, elle exhale le *Oui* suprême.' [8]

This paragraph sums up the entire action of the work. It is the great theme which runs through the plays of Claudel, *L'Annonce*, *L'Otage*, *Le Soulier de satin*: the restoration of unity and harmony through sacrifice freely accepted, and the joy which results. In *L'Otage* the sacrifice is imperfectly accepted and the drama ends in ambiguity and pain instead of peace and joy.

It is clear that such had been Claudel's concept of Jeanne d'Arc's mission at least since the composition of *L'Annonce*, some twenty years earlier. Exactly when the second version of *La Jeune Fille Violaine* was transformed in its author's imagination into *L'Annonce* with its medieval setting and the background figure of Jeanne d'Arc is unclear. Two events were no doubt of importance however in attracting Claudel's attention to Jeanne and her period. The first was the beatification in 1909, the second the publication of Péguy's *Mystère de la charité de Jeanne d'Arc* which Gide sent to him in February 1910. In February 1909 Claudel had refused to allow *La Jeune Fille Violaine* to be performed at the Nouveau Théâtre d'Art, and in letters to Gide and Suarès he gave among his reasons the fact that he would wish to supervise the production himself, this play being 'ma pièce la plus intime, la moins extérieurement séduisante'.[9] No doubt the problem sent him back to his play, and to Gide he confided that he was thinking of eliminating the role of Pierre de Craon, but he had apparently not yet thought of transferring the action to another historical period. By December 1910 he mentions to Gide that he is working hard on a new version (Prague, 22 December 1910), and by February 1911 he has found the title *L'Annonce faite à Marie*. He was also working hard on *L'Otage* during this period, and in that play also there is a reminiscence of Jeanne d'Arc. Sygne is called to a mission parallel to Jeanne's, the healing of division through personal sacrifice. In her flows the blood of 'celui-là de nos ancêtres qui combattit contre Jeanne avec le Bourguignon, et de celui-là qui se fit renégat' (III, ii, p. 283), Sygne's vocation is to make reparation for the ancestral fault, to sacrifice herself in the cause of unity and order, to save the Pope and bring about the union of the old and new France by her marriage with the detestable Turelure. As her acceptance is not whole-hearted, her success is incomplete. None the less the restoration of the King at the end of the play does seem to indicate, as in *L'Annonce* and *Jeanne au bûcher*, that order and unity of some sort are indeed restored through Sygne's efforts.

In *L'Annonce* three figures are closely linked, the Blessed Virgin, Violaine and Jeanne d'Arc. The vocation of the two latter figures could be called an *imitatio Mariae* and the parallel is made evident in the fact that their obedience to vocation, like hers, bears fruit in the night of Christmas, when the Christ child is born, the dead child is restored to life and the King is crowned at Rheims. As the fruit of sacrifice accepted, joy is born again into the world, death, the wages of sin, is overcome, divisions are healed and unity restored. As the Virgin Mary is called to co-operate in the work of redemption, in the restoration of unity between God and man which Adam's sin had destroyed, so Violaine the contemplative and Jeanne d'Arc in her call to the active life co-operate in the expiation of the sins of the world. By their obedience and sacrifice the disorders in the Church and divisions in the kingdom are healed, the evils of war overcome. Violaine explains her vocation thus:

> Ils n'ont point de père. Ils regardent et ne savent plus où est le Roi et le Pape.
>
> C'est pourquoi voici mon corps en travail à la place de la chrétienté qui se dissout.
>
> Puissante est la souffrance quand elle est aussi volontaire que le péché!
>
> (III, iii, p. 75

The play ends in the peace of harmony restored, of sin forgiven, and Anne Vercors accepts tranquilly the death of Violaine:

> . . . Ma femme aussi
>
> Est morte, ma fille est morte, la sainte Pucelle
>
> A été brûlée et jetée au vent, pas un de ses os ne reste à la terre.
>
> Mais le Roi et le Pontife de nouveau sont rendus à la France et à l'Univers.
>
> (IV, v, p. 104)

Claudel's concept of Jeanne d'Arc's life and death did not change between 1910 and 1939. *Jeanne au bûcher* has clearly grown from *L'Annonce*; the concept of sainthood as at once an *imitatio Christi* (the passion) and an *imitatio Mariae* (the vocation) is illustrated by Violaine in the first work and by Jeanne in the second. Parallels between Jeanne and Violaine are numerous. Both are peasant girls, delighting in the beauty of the countryside, touched by the simplicity of folksong (*Marguerite de Paris* for Violaine, Trimazô's song for Jeanne). Both follow in the footsteps of the

71

early martyrs; the relics of the child martyr Justitia are in the foundations of Pierre de Craon's church while Violaine's ring shines in the spire (thus is the Church founded upon and glorified in the sacrifice of her saints) and Jeanne too follows the martyrs and is 'livrée aux bêtes' (sc. iv). Violaine is consumed by leprosy as Jeanne is consumed by fire, and the leprosy is frequently described metaphorically as fire in *L'Annonce*; the symbol of sin in the case of Pierre de Craon, leprosy is the mark of God's all-consuming love in Violaine, not destroying but liberating; Violaine says:

> Le bois où l'on a mis le feu ne donne pas de la cendre seulement mais une flamme aussi
>
> (III, iii, p. 74)

while in *Jeanne au bûcher* the choir sings:

> Loué soit/notre frère le feu/qui est puissant à rendre l'esprit et cendre – cendre – cendre,/ce qui est cendre à la terre.
>
> (sc. xi, p. 1225)

Scene vii of *Jeanne au bûcher*, the scene of peasant rejoicing for the coronation of the Dauphin, is a clear transposition of Act III of *L'Annonce*. The two colossal carnival figures have become Heurtebise and La Mère aux Tonneaux, while the workers clearing a road through the forest have become a joyful band of peasants. Mara's reading of Isaiah, the homilies and the gospel is replaced by the choir chanting the psalm *Adspiciens a longe* . . . and of course the coming of the Messiah, fruit of Mary's vocation, is reflected in the arrival of the King at Rheims on Christmas day, the culmination of Jeanne's mission. The allegory of Nature, the message of hope and fruitfulness in the seasons and their renewal, the bond of unity between man and nature, one creation, enriches the symbolism and metaphors of both works.

Claudel's saint is only *Jeanne d'Arc parvenue à l'auréole* in the last moments of the work and it is hardly exact when he says he has not tried to depict *la petite paysanne*. The pathos, youth and innocence of the victim are underlined throughout, whether in

Jeanne's naïve questioning of Frère Dominique or when she recalls
the earliest moment of her vocation at Domrémy:

> Je les reconnais! La Catherine qui dit *De profundis*/et la
> Marguerite bleue et blanche dans le ciel qui dit *Papa Maman*!
>
> Comme je les écoutais jadis à Domrémy, la Catherine et la
> Marguerite!
>
> Jhésus! Marie! j'ai écrit ces deux noms sur ma jolie bannière
> bleue et blanche.
>
> Jhésus! Marie!
>
> Catherine! Marguerite!
>
> Et moi; ce petit bout de femme dans les orties et les boutons
> d'or, si ébahie qu'elle oubliait de manger sa tartine.
>
> (sc. vii, p. 1213)

This touching image of Jeanne, emphasizing her childlike
qualities, the compassion which inspired her action, the poetic
association of the 'Voices' with church bells, has of course
historical authority. While not seeking to emulate the historian,
Claudel was acquainted with the facts and in a talk given at Basle
in 1938 for the first *Jeanne au bûcher*[10] he recapitulates and comments upon them, making all the major ideas of his oratorio
explicit. The villains in the drama he names as Pierre Cauchon,
Jean le Maître who was the Dominican vice-inquisitor ('qui
paraît avoir été surtout un lâche'), and behind them the 'grand
coupable', the University of Paris, motivated by spiritual and
intellectual pride, outraged in its pretentions by Jeanne's claims,
daring to raise itself even against the Pope, furthering its own ends
at the councils of Constance and Basle, willing to believe that
Jeanne was an agent of the devil but ruling out all possibility
that God could be on the other side. All this is in the oratorio.
Frère Dominique says:

> Tous ces grands hommes qui t'ont condamnée, ces docteurs
> et ces savants,
> Malvenu,/Jean Midi,/Coupequesne et Toutmouillé,
> Ils croient dur au Diable, mais ils ne veulent pas croire à Dieu.
> . . .

Telle est la sagesse de la Sorbonne.

Tels sont ces illustres docteurs qui donnent des nazardes au Pape.

(sc. vi; p.1209–1210)

Claudel underlines Jeanne's orthodoxy, her appeal (disallowed) to Pope and Council, her moment of fear and human weakness at the abjuration, her recovery and heroic death. He is clearly acquainted in some detail with the evidence of both trials. He may at some time have looked at the invaluable five volumes of documents published by Quicherat (1841–9) which are on the open shelves of the Bibliothèque Nationale (Claudel held a reader's ticket from 1886),[11] or he may have seen Pierre Champion's two-volume edition of the documents of Rouen, published in 1921.[12] Not only the lecture of 1938, but also the names cited in *Jeanne au bûcher* show a degree of familiarity with the proceedings of 1431 – Malvenue, Jean Midi, Coupequesne et Toutmouillé – names chosen no doubt because they are slightly grotesque. Two details have been deliberately changed: Jean Midi was actually Nicolas Midi, but the correct Christian name would ruin the hemistich. Malvenu was in fact Ladvenu: the change makes the name more baleful. Similarly Cauchon became Cochon: the pun was much too good to miss, especially given the value which Claudel attributes to words and their relationships in the *Art Poétique*.

The documents of the Rehabilitation were until recently much less accessible than those of 1431, but biographies of Jeanne d'Arc indebted to them were of course numerous. Like many historians favourable to Jeanne and inclined to believe that she was indeed supernaturally inspired, Claudel's view is markedly formed by the picture which emerges from the documents of 1456. It is to the witnesses at that trial that we are indebted for the details of Jeanne's childhood and for the testimony of her friends in Charles VII's army, captains such as Dunois, La Hire, Alençon. All these witnesses testify to her piety, charity, goodness, even ignorance (she was illiterate), thus underlining the supernatural aspect of her success. Some of the members of the court of Rouen also appeared and proved anxious to throw all the odium of the first trial onto the now dead Cauchon. The trial of 1456 is generally denigrated by sceptical or anti-clerical historians, such as Anatole France, who refuse to see in it anything but a stroke of political propaganda, while on the other hand they make every effort to exonerate the judges of 1431, conveniently overlooking the tremendous and vital propaganda value of that trial for the Anglo-Burgundian cause. Shaw followed this line, while Claudel, like Michelet, is indebted to the witnesses of 1456. So also is that other great Michelet-admirer Charles Péguy, whose Hauviette in the *Mystère de la charité de Jeanne d'Arc* existed in fact and lived to testify at the Rehabilitation.

Michelet is probably the seminal influence in Claudel's concept of Jeanne's life. The attention with which he had at some time read Michelet's account is evident from a letter of 28 September 1912 to Gide in which he remarks that 'Michelet, avec sa finesse maladive, avait remarqué que les Anglais souvent ont le sens de Satan (lui l'avait aussi). Thomas de Quincey avait relevé cette remarque.'[13] This is almost certainly not an allusion to *La Sorcière*, as R. Mallet suggests, but to the remarks in Chapter V of *Jeanne d'Arc*. Th. de Quincey took them up in an article entitled 'Joan of Arc' published in *Tait's Magazine* for March–August 1847.[14]

Michelet, Claudel and Péguy all see Jeanne as the peasant girl whose heart was touched by 'la grande pitié qu'il y avait au royaume de France', inspired in her mission by a great charity. Claudel follows Michelet in implying that Jeanne considered her work finished at Rheims (this is not historically accurate) and that the time had come for her to take stock spiritually. Michelet writes: 'Elle avait dit en parlant de la délivrance d'Orléans et du sacre de Reims: "C'est pour cela que je suis née." Ces deux choses accomplies, sa sainteté était en péril' (Ch. III). Claudel also follows Michelet in suggesting that Jeanne was betrayed at Compiègne by the captain of the place, Flavy. As mentioned earlier, this is historically extremely doubtful. Claudel and Michelet agree again on the iniquity of Cauchon, the pusillanimity of the court. It is in the significance of the trial itself that they part company, for Michelet sees in it the conflict between 'd'une part, l'Église visible et l'autorité, de l'autre, l'inspiration attestant l'Église invisible' (Ch. IV). This is not far from Shaw's Protestant saint, who drew down upon the heretical Irishman's head the ire of Claudel ('Un écrivain asburde, qui aurait mieux fait de rester fidèle à ses clowneries habituelles'!)[15] Claudel and Michelet are reconciled again however in the significance they accord to the actual moment of Jeanne's death; Michelet writes:

> Que toute incertitude ait cessé dans les flammes, cela nous doit faire croire qu'elle accepta la mort pour la *délivrance* promise, qu'elle n'entendit plus le *salut* au sens judaïque et matériel, comme elle avait fait jusque-là, qu'elle vit clair enfin, et que, sortant des ombres, elle obtint ce qui lui manquait encore de lumière et de sainteté (Ch. VI).

The whole concept of *Jeanne au bûcher* could be summed up in that sentence.

Claudel is not an historian, but a poet who has a religious view of history. Because the view is religious, he has a respect for events, seeing in them the evidence of God's ways to man; being a poet, he reserves to himself the manner of presentation: selection of those aspects rich in significance, replacement of the contingent by the symbolic. All the anecdotal and epic elements of the story are omitted, the recognition scene in Chinon, the liberation of Orléans. Only the moments which illuminate Jeanne's vocation and its meaning are considered: Rouen, Rheims, Domrémy. We are led in a circular movement from the darkness to the light that, having better understood the darkness, we may return and vanquish it. To create this aesthetically and morally satisfying pattern the chronological order of events is reversed. Events are respected, but the contingent detail gives way to the greater claims of spiritual truth, conveyed by symbol and metaphor. Thus the date of the coronation is altered from 17 July to 25 December in order to point the meaning of sanctity in general and of Jeanne's vocation in particular. No doubt also Claudel was well aware that

Jeanne did not consider her mission accomplished at Rheims and that France was not reunited immediately; artistically he is justified in suggesting the contrary, for his presentation of events is not a contradiction of history but a condensation. Fidelity to the letter would be detrimental both to the spirit of history and to the requirements of art, for Rheims itself has here the value of a symbol, representing the ultimate conquest of the forces of disorder and evil by the force of love and sacrifice. There is no conflict in the spectator's reaction to the change, for it is clear on which level it is to be taken; the figures of Heurtebise and La Mère aux Tonneaux place the whole scene on the level of symbol. There is no crisis of credibility such as is liable to occur when alterations in historical fact are presented on the plane of psychological or factual realism. The second deliberate change in fact is of the same nature: Jeanne declares that she has found her sword not in a ruined church but in Domrémy. As previously, the major fact (the coronation, the finding of a sword) is left intact, the contingent detail (date, place) is altered to increase the value of the symbol.

Throughout the work historic truth is examined in the light of spiritual truth. The symbolism springs from the events, be it Rheims or Jeanne's death in the month of May. But the perspective of the work is given in its opening and conclusion, which are taken entirely outside the confines of history and set in the light of eternity by the appearance of the two heavenly patrons, St Dominic and the Virgin Mary, one leading Jeanne through the events of her life, the other encouraging and receiving her at the moment of death, which is the moment of victory. Each of the two represents also the eternal justice of God in which all wrongs are righted, all injuries redressed. As the Dominicans had played a major part at Rouen it was necessary that the misdeeds of 1431 should be condemned by the founder of the order; as Jeanne had been faithful to her vocation, as she too was the handmaid of the Lord, *Pucelle de Dieu*, it was fitting that the Queen of All Saints should receive into heaven *Sainte Jeanne parvenue à l'auréole*. The Virgin who appears at the end of *Jeanne au bûcher* is not the

Reine des Sept douleurs, much less the poor grief-stricken peasant woman of Péguy's *Mystère*, and one can readily understand why Claudel had reservations about such a picture. For him, Mary is above all the *Queen assumed into Heaven*, our guarantee of ultimate victory, joy and the wiping away of all tears. His concept of heaven is the triumphant vision of Rubens, of the Counter-Reformation. *Jeanne d'Arc au bûcher*, which had opened in darkness and desolation rent by the doleful howl of the evil spirit, ends in the apotheosis of a dawn resplendent with heavenly voices as the martyr's sacrifice is consumated in joy and love.

NOTES

1. Paul Claudel, 'Sur Jeanne d'Arc'. Lecture given at Basle in 1938 and published in *Les Cahiers du Rhône II. Cahier de Poésie*, Neufchâtel: Eds. de la Baconnière, 1942, p. 36.
2. Page numbers are from *Théâtre II*, Pl., Paris, 1959.
3. See Martin le Franc's *Champion des Dames*, c. 1440; published in Quicherat: *Procès de Condamnation et de Réhabilitation de Jeanne d'Arc*, t. V., Paris, 1841-9, 5 vol.
4. See the interview given by Claudel to *Germania*, 10.4.1926, quoted by L. Chaigne in *Vie de Paul Claudel et genèse de son oeuvre*, Paris: Mame, 1961, p. 185.
5. 'Sainte Jeanne d'Arc', in *Visages Radieux. Poésies*, Pl., Paris, 1957, pp. 808-11.
6. L. Chaigne, op. cit., pp. 8-9.
7. 'Sur Jeanne d'Arc', op. cit., pp. 23 and 24.
8. ibid., pp. 36-7.
9. *André Suarès et Paul Claudel. Correspondance, 1904-1938*, Paris: Gallimard, 1951, pp. 142-3. *Paul Claudel et André Gide. Correspondance, 1899-1926*, Paris: Gallimard, 1949, pp. 98-9.
10. op. cit.
11. See A. Vachon, *Le Temps et l'espace dans l'oeuvre de Claudel*, Paris: Editions du Seuil, 1965, p. 68.
12. P. Champion, *Procès de condamnation de Jeanne d'Arc* (2 vols.), Paris: Champion, 1921. It was exhibit no. 517 in the Claudel exhibition of 1968 at the Bibliothèque Nationale.
13. *Paul Claudel et André Gide. Correspondance*, p. 204.
14. See Rudler's edition, Paris, 1925. De Quincey's essay was reprinted in his *Collected Writings*, t. 3, 1854.
15. 'Sur Jeanne d'Arc', op. cit., p. 23.

6 · The *Cinq grandes odes* of Paul Claudel[1]

EDWARD LUCIE-SMITH

> And will pardon Paul Claudel,
> Pardons him for writing well.

THUS W. H. Auden, in the old version of his poem 'In Memory of W. B. Yeats'. The lines have disappeared from the recently published *Collected Poems*. Nevertheless, they remain the most famous reference to Claudel's work by an English or American author. More, they seem to reflect pretty accurately the views of those Englishmen who have heard of Claudel at all.

Auden, writing in 1939, couples Claudel with Kipling. They are both, for him, authoritarians, arch-reactionaries. It is certainly true that there is an authoritarian, a deliberately conformist streak in Claudel's character. Yet it would be a mistake to think of him, any more than of Kipling, as a man who effortlessly fitted into an existing establishment. Both were too vehement, too inflexible for that. For example, there is Claudel's Catholicism, perhaps the most important thing in his life, and certainly a dominant element in his poetry. The Anglo-Saxon reader is disconcerted by Claudel's almost frantic insistence upon his own doctrinal orthodoxy:

> Je crois sans y changer un seul point ce que mes pères ont cru avant moi,
> Confessant le Sauveur des hommes et Jésus qui est mort sur la croix,
>
> ('Processional pour saluer le siècle nouveau')

Of course, this is in part at least due to a misunderstanding. We forget, never having experienced anything like it in our own recent history, the ferocious secularism to be found in the France of the period, and the official backing which it received. Claudel says with reason:

79

> Tous les hommes alors étaient contre nous et je ne répondais
> rien, la science, la raison.
>
> ('La Maison fermée')

He describes how:

> Ainsi jadis dans cette ville impie de la Bourgogne j'ai vu la
> statue abattue de Notre-Dame, gisante la face contre terre
> sous la neige, suppliante pour l'iniquité de son peuple . . .
>
> ('La Maison fermée')

We also forget the feverish climate of the whole epoch. For
example, Claudel's denunciation, in 'Magnificat', of 'vos "génies"
et vos "héros", vos grands hommes et vos surhommes' recalls to
us at once the fact that he was the contemporary, not only of
Kaiser Wilhelm II, but of d'Annunzio and of the Italian Futurists.
To be an orthodox Catholic in the intellectual and political
climate of the time was therefore, in a real sense, an act of non-
conformity, and Claudel's insistence on the faith must be considered in that light.

True, matters of religion apart, Claudel the career diplomat
seems a far from Bohemian figure, though we are told that he
disconcerted his superior by ignoring Talleyrand's famous piece
of advice to young diplomats: 'surtout pas trop de zèle'. But it is
at least conceivable that the man who so openly gloried in his
talents as an administrator, who positively revelled in being a 'bon
fonctionnaire' was playing a role. One of the most significant
lines in the whole text of the *Cinq grandes odes* is the cry:

> Je suis libre, délivrez-moi de la liberté!
>
> ('L'Esprit et L'Eau')

It would be foolish to pretend that Claudel's character is not an
unexpected one in a modern poet. There is, for instance, his entire
lack of flexibility when confronted with the experience offered
to him by China. Of the three great poets who wrote at about the
same time concerning their experience of Asia – Claudel,
Segalen and St-John Perse – Claudel is by far the least seduced.

There is a splendid evocation of Peking and the surrounding plain at the beginning of 'L'Esprit et L'Eau':

> C'est ainsi que dans le vieux vent de la Terre, la Cité carrée dresse ses retranchements et ses portes,
>
> Étage ses Portes colossales dans le vent jaune, trois fois trois portes comme des éléphants,
>
> Dans le vent de cendre et de poussière, dans le grand vent gris de la poudre qui fut Sodome, et les empires d'Égypte et des Perses, et Paris, et Tadmor, et Babylone.

But this must be balanced against his frequent disapproving references to Chinese customs, and especially to Chinese religion. Japan, where he was later to be ambassador, pleased him more, or so we may guess from the *Cent Phrases pour Éventails*. Segalen remarks, in his *Lettres de Chine*,[2] that Claudel 'méprise un peu le caractère chinois. La médiocrité, la moyenne y est sans doute un peu plus élevée qu'en Europe, mais aucune "tête". Ce qui fait la supériorité occidentale, c'est qu'elle possède à chaque génération cinquante hommes hors pair.' Segalen also reports, in the same passage, Claudel's total ignorance of Chinese. But none of these observations can possibly impugn Claudel's right to be considered fundamentally 'modernist' in his way of thinking and writing.

For the English-speaking reader, the most illuminating comparison is probably that with Wallace Stevens, that other untypical 'modernist'. Stevens the successful insurance man has at first sight much in common with the French diplomat-poet. He too was content with his lot, and enjoyed his career rather than chafing at it; he too was rather a late starter as a poet; he too was a conservative in politics. There are also deeper resemblances. Stevens's essential gaudiness of language is the equivalent in English of Claudel's rhetoric. It's almost as if the freedom, the energy, the lack of economy in the use of language, the prodigality with imagery, spring from the security which the writer himself enjoyed.

But the differences are just as important as the resemblances.

Claudel the believer must be contrasted with Stevens the sceptic. 'Sunday Morning' might almost have been written as a mocking reply to the picture which Claudel gives in the *Cinq grandes odes* of a 'closed' universe, entirely permeated by the divine spirit.

This concept, moreover, is one which springs directly from Claudel's own character. Gide called him 'un cyclone figé' (a congealed tornado). Yet here again the poems are 'modernist' in that they bear very directly upon the writer's own preoccupations. They are confessions, in the sense that modern poetry has been so since Baudelaire. It is interesting to see what one learns from the *Odes* about the poet himself, and his personal existence. For instance, though early in the list of the poet's works, the poems are not the creation of a very young man. In some respects, they are a response to the feeling that the poet is already growing old:

> Car l'année qui fut celle-là
> Quand je commençai à voir le feuillage se décomposer et l'incendie du monde prendre,
> Pour échapper aux saisons le soir frais me parut une aurore, l'automne le printemps d'une lumière plus fixe,
> Je le suivis comme une armée qui se retire en brûlant tout derrière elle. Toujours
> Plus avant jusqu'au cœur de la mer luisante!
>
> ('Les Muses')

They represent a kind of moral and spiritual crisis which usually comes earlier in a man's life if he is going to suffer it at all. Claudel spent his thirties in meeting the storms which are more easily weathered by men of twenty. Not that his early manhood had been entirely uneventful. One of the central events in the *Cinq grandes odes* is the fact of Claudel's conversion (for he did not arrive at religion by gradual steps).

By one of the paradoxes which abound in Claudel's work, this conversion, which took place in 1886, was prepared for by a reading of Rimbaud, whose work Claudel had first encountered in the same year. He was later to describe Rimbaud as 'un mystique à l'état sauvage'. The marvellous description of the moment of conversion in 'Magnificat':

> Et je fus devant vous comme un lutteur qui plie,
> Non qu'il se croie faible, mais parce que l'autre est plus fort.

might perhaps also be applied to the relationship between Claudel's talent as a writer and Rimbaud's. There is a real sense in which Claudel earned his place in the pantheon which also includes Baudelaire, Mallarmé and Valéry, by being the first to seize upon the universal elements in Rimbaud's work. He saw that here was not merely an explosion of genius in a quarter even more unexpected than usual, but a new way of handling language and imagery.

The point of contact between Rimbaud and Catholicism in Claudel's mind lay precisely in the idea of the symbolic. Wallace Fowlie says, in his little book on Claudel, that 'Claudel learned from the example of Baudelaire and Rimbaud the lesson of "pure receptivity", a state in which language will be far less an expression through words than a revelation of meaning through symbols'.[3] Rimbaud's doctrine of the *voyant* is transformed by Claudel into something different, but closely related. For Claudel the word is the Logos, and the poet's words celebrate and recreate the universe of God. To this he adds the Thomist idea that everything has existed from the beginning in the mind of God. Hence, as Fowlie notes: 'The creation is the poem conceived in the mind of God'.[4] Hence, too, the Claudelian tendency to reconcile movement and stasis, which may remind us of a similar phenomenon in modern music.

The method offers the poet a number of advantages. Basing himself on these ideas, Claudel was able to universalise particular experiences, and to relate the events of a single life (his own) to the energies of the world. Erato, at the end of 'Les Muses', is the woman Claudel loved and could not possess, just as Ysé in *Partage de midi* is the same woman. He met her on his return to his post in China in 1901, after a period in France when he had failed to find a vocation as a priest: Claudel manages to give this love-affair on shipboard genuine depth of meaning; it becomes one of the central symbols of his work, without losing any of its human qualities. Characteristic is the way that the images work in these lines, taken from the passage I am talking about. The personal and the universal are intertwined:

> Toi-même, amie, tes grands cheveux blonds dans le vent de la mer,
> Tu n'as pas su les tenir bien serrés sur ta tête; ils s'effondrent! les lourds anneaux
> Roulent sur tes épaules, la grande chose joconde
> S'enlève, tout part dans le clair de la lune!
> Et les étoiles ne sont-elles point pareilles à des têtes d'épingles luisantes? et tout l'édifice du monde ne fait-il pas une splendeur aussi fragile
> Qu'une royale chevelure de femme prête à crouler sous le peigne!

('Les Muses')

It may be said that it requires a very considerable egotism to mythologize one's own life in this fashion. Claudel was conscious of this to the point where he often withheld works from publication, or gave them a limited circulation only. He only gave permission for *Partage de midi* to be published in a commercial edition and publicly performed in 1948. He had initially intended to delay this until after his own death. Claudel himself once confessed: 'Many men are proud, but know better how to hide it than I have done.' When considering the matter of Claudel's egotism, and whether or not this mars his work, it is as well to look at the correspondence with Gide. Claudel remarks at one point: 'A Catholic has no allies, he can only have brothers.' And this is the secret (another Claudelian paradox) why the extreme concentration of the self which we find in the *Odes* often makes them universal.

But the man who could make poetry work for him in this way did indeed have to be a special sort of human being – one with an appetite for experiences which went beyond the common.

Claudel, because he is a Catholic, is unwilling to leave any event, any phenomenon to one side. His poems, being Catholic poems, must correspond to his idea of the Church: 'The Church is anything but exclusive because it is Catholic; that is to say universal and leaving absolutely nothing outside itself.' There is humility as well as ambition in Claudel – he feels he has no right *not* to attempt the largest. The voraciousness and the massive self-exposure of his work are the two qualities which make him in a sense the real opposite to Mallarmé, the other term of the poetic proposition. We get a glimpse of what he was after in his remark that: 'The best poetry of the nineteenth century is a poetry of revolt. But after all, revolt has great disadvantages. It doesn't take you anywhere.' Revolt for Claudel also implied a sort of defensiveness. Gingerly he might sometimes be about publication, but by design he was the least self-defensive of writers.

Having thus tried to give a general idea of the kind of context into which the *Cinq grandes odes* may be fitted, and their general tenor, I should now like to look a little more closely into the way in which each of them works as poetry. Claudel called them: 'True symphonies, developing not in continuous sequence in the literary manner, but orchestrally, with themes interlaced and varied.' The prosody of the *Odes* is calculated to support this 'musical' view of poetry – the lines, or *versets*, respond in length and weight to the content of meaning, and within the line lives the breath of the poet, rising, falling, gathering speed or losing it. Charles Olson's doctrine of 'projective verse', now so fashionable in America, has a forerunner in Claudel, just as the notion of poetic immediacy helps to link Claudel to Allen Ginsberg.

The physical sweep, the breadth of rhythm in the *Odes*, matches, and even on occasion out-matches, the breadth of intellectual range. But the ode, in its classical incarnation, always permitted the poet a certain abruptness – Claudel must certainly have noted effects of this sort in Pindar – and, in his use of abrupt transitions, he manages to make tradition and modernity march in step.

Of all the five poems, the one which is most clearly different from the rest of the sequence is the first, 'Les Muses'. It stands in about the same relation to the rest as 'Du côté de chez Swann' does to the rest of *A la recherche du temps perdu*. It has often been observed that this first book in Proust's immense work is more finely and delicately written than the rest – I think that much the same could be said about 'Les Muses'. There is nothing in the other odes which quite matches the lyricism of the passage describing Erato which I have already quoted, and there is very little to match the melancholy dignity of the farewell to Homer, to Virgil and to Dante:

> Et d'abord on ne voyait que leur miroir infini, mais soudain sous la propagation de l'immense sillage,
> Elles s'animent et le monde entier se peint sur l'étoffe magique.

On the other hand, of all the poems, this is the one whose construction seems much the stiffest. The poet takes for his theme the Muses as they now appear on a famous sarcophagus found on the road to Ostia, and now in the Louvre. Each muse is spoken of in turn; her attributes are described, and these pagan beings are brought into relationship with the universe of God. But there is something a little mechanical about this, and an ode burdened with so much classical apparatus sometimes cannot escape from pastiche.

In the next poem, Claudel has already freed himself from these trammels. 'L'Esprit et L'Eau' begins with the poet looking out from the walls of Peking. The dry and dusty land of North China becomes a metaphor for spiritual aridity. This is perhaps the poem where the universality of the poet's concern shows itself most clearly, as in the curious metaphor where he compares himself to the oceans drawing the rivers into themselves:

> Si j'étais la mer, crucifiée par un milliard de bras sur ses deux continents,
> A plein ventre ressentant la traction rude du ciel circulaire avec le soleil immobile comme la mèche allumée sous la ventouse,

Connaissant ma propre quantité,
C'est moi, je tire, j'appelle sur tout mes racines, le Gange, le Mississippi,
L'épaisse touffe de l'Orénoque, le long fil du Rhin, le Nil avec sa double vessie,
Et le lion nocturne buvant, et les marais, et les vases souterrains, et le cœur rond et plein des hommes qui durent leur instant.

On the other hand, just because he is so concerned with the theological and universal aspect, Claudel sometimes lets theology triumph over his concern for the density of poetic language, and the poem has stretches which are linguistically rather inert.

This fault is to be found again in 'Magnificat' which, together with 'La Maison fermée', seems to me the least successful of the five poems. 'Magnificat' is Claudel's thanksgiving for his conversion, and it is somewhat disconcerting to find the praise mingled with so many denunciations of those whom he despises:

Ne me perdez point avec les Voltaire, et les Renan, et les Michelet, et les Hugo, et tout les autres infâmes!
Leur âme est avec les chiens morts, leur livres sont joints au fumier.
Ils sont morts, et leur nom même après leur mort est un poison et une pourriture.

But this at least is vigorous. It is in 'Magnificat' that Claudel's rhetoric comes nearest to flaccidity. The English reader is perhaps more sensitive to this than a French one might be, because Claudel bases himself so much upon the language of the Bible, which for obvious historical reasons subsumes the English classics to a far greater extent than French ones. A translator becomes acutely aware of this difficulty. In rendering 'Magnificat' into English I found that I was constantly on the brink of a rather limp imitation of the language of the Authorised Version, and that sometimes, out of the desire to be faithful to the author, I was forced to submit entirely. Yet Claudel is capable of grappling even with these difficulties—he makes a fine thing of the passage at the end of the poem which describes Joshua descending towards the Promised Land:

> Après la longue montée, après les longues étapes dans la neige et dans la nuée,
> Il est comme un homme qui commence à descendre, tenant de la main droite son cheval par le bridon.
> Et ses femmes sont avec lui en arrière sur les chevaux et les ânes, et les enfants dans les bâts et le matériel de guerre et du campement, et les Tables de la Loi sont par derrière,
> Et il entend derrière lui dans le brouillard le bruit de tout un peuple qui marche.

Like most poets, Claudel is at his best with the concretely visualized.

The fourth poem, 'La Muse qui est la Grâce', is to me the most impressive of the entire series. There are a number of reasons for this. In language it is almost, if not quite, as finely wrought as the first of the *Odes*. Claudel speaks of the approach of inspiration with magical delicacy:

> Et je suis comme la jeune fille à la fenetre du beau chateau blanc, dans le clair de lune,
> Qui entend, le cœur bondissant, ce bienheureux sifflement sous les arbres et le bruit de deux chevaux qui s'agitent,
> Et elle ne regrette point la maison, mais elle est comme un petit tigre qui se ramasse, et tout son cœur est soulevé par l'amour de la vie et par la grande force cosmique!

But the real reason for the success of the poem lies in the form Claudel has adopted. He reverts to the classical pattern of strophe and antistrophe, and turns it into a debate between the poet and the Muse. We are made aware of the divisions within the writer himself. The poet resists the transcendental. As the argument prefaced to the poem tells us: 'le poéte bouche les oreilles et se retourne vers la terre':

Va-t'en! tu ne m'ôteras point ce froid goût de la terre,
Cette obstination avec la terre qu'il y a dans la moelle
de mes os et dans le caillou de ma substance et dans le noir
noyau de mes viscères!

This harsh rejection, even of Grace itself, tells us a truth which we
have in any case already sensed about Claudel's character, and the
revelation is the more moving for that.

In this respect, the fifth ode, 'La Maison fermée', makes a contrast with the one which immediately precedes it. This is the least
pleasing of the poems, because there is about it an air of smugness.
Mauriac reproached Claudel, when replying to the discourse
which the latter made on his admission to the Académie Française,
with 'sometimes letting your colleagues perceive, by an air of
excessive jubilation, that it is you who will last out to the end, that
you will laugh on your last day, and that the thought that they
themselves will be consigned to eternal flames is not disagreeable
to you'. True, the world outside is permitted to have its say:

Poéte, tu nous trahis! Porte-parole, où portes-tu cette
parole que nous t'avons confiée?

Claudel replies to this question much in the spirit of a rebellious
English Member of Parliament informing his constituency that
he is, after all, not their delegate, but merely their representative,
and that he will therefore speak as he pleases in the House of
Commons. His joy in his new-found domesticity, his celebration
of wife and children, these remind one more than a little of the
sentimental Coventry Patmore whom Claudel translated. The
apparatus in this ode seems a little too massive for the content.

I have spoken at some length of the flaws to be found in the
Cinq grandes odes. Certainly Claudel is not a 'perfect' poet – but
then his ambition was rather different from that – he aimed to be
great rather than perfect. Despite his denunciation of 'geniuses'
and 'heroes' his final aim was to be ranked among their number.
The solemnity of this ambition is something rather unusual among
modern poets, who have approached the question of greatness

with a distinctly nervous tread – witness, for example, the tactical manœuvrings undertaken by T. S. Eliot in both *The Waste Land* and *Four Quartets*. The significant word in the title given to the odes is undoubtedly the adjective, and it is up to the reader to decide whether it is justified. There is an ambiguous epigram coined by Claudel himself which seems to suit the case: 'Quelqu'un qui admire a toujours raison'. Arrogant Claudel is, and sometimes inflated or clumsy. But for me the *Cinq grandes odes* remain admirable enough to justify most of the claims their creator made for them.

NOTES

1. Some parts of this essay, differently arranged, appeared as the preface to my translation of the *Cinq grandes odes*, London: Rapp & Whiting, 1967.
2. Victor Segalen, *Lettres de Chine*, Paris: Plon, 1967.
3. Wallace Fowlie, *Paul Claudel*, London: Bowes & Bowes, 1957, p. 38.
4. ibid., p. 50.

Part two · More evidence on Claudel

7 · Claudel and Sophia

ERNEST BEAUMONT

CLAUDEL IS ONE of the very few imaginative writers in whose work Sophia, or Divine Wisdom, plays a substantial role. Indeed, it is a theological notion which has been little developed in the West, though it figures prominently in the Christian thought of the East. According to C. G. Jung, the idea of Sophia, which has its origin in the Book of Proverbs, in particular the eighth chapter, is a symptom of Greek influence in the Bible, though he also points to its close association with the Hebrew Chochma and is himself reminded by it of the Indian Shakti. Jung defines the notion as 'a coeternal and more or less hypostatized pneuma of feminine nature that existed before the Creation', quoting the relevant verses from Proverbs 8.[1] It seems that in the early Church the figure of Sophia was identified sometimes with the Holy Spirit, sometimes with the Logos, but, in the fourteenth century, with the development of St Gregory Palamas's doctrine of the uncreated energies, Wisdom came to be regarded as divine energy, manifested in the Son and communicated in the Holy Spirit. It was through and in Sophia that God created the universe.[2] That is why, according to Olivier Clément, Wisdom was represented symbolically as a winged woman of grave beauty, behind whom there was often silhouetted a seven-columned structure deriving from Proverbs 9: i.[3] In Russian theological speculation in modern times the idea of Sophia has been notably developed by Solovyov, Florensky and Bulgakov, the latter in fact incurring censure for having, so it was alleged, postulated the feminine principle within the Godhead Itself.[4] Obviously, the feminine figure of the Book of Proverbs exerts its influence, naturally enough, on theological understanding of the notion of Divine Wisdom. It is, however, important to establish that, in sophiological thinking, particularly as exemplified by Bulgakov, the most subtle as well as in some ways the most extreme sophiologist, there are two Sophias: the divine Sophia, uncreated Wisdom, and the creaturely Sophia, created Wisdom. Christ manifests the hypostatic image of the former, the Virgin Mary is the created hypostasis of the creaturely Sophia, though Christ in fact unites in his nature, in the hypostatic union of Godhead and manhood, both Sophias. It was Mary, however, the created hypostasis of the creaturely Sophia, who gave the Logos his human nature, his birth being accomplished physically and spiritually through her. She is, as it were, the perfect image of created Wisdom by itself. From this premise and from her overshadowing by the Holy Spirit who rests eternally on the Logos and brings Mary with him into himself, Bulgakov argues in *Agnus Dei* that the birth of God was the spiritual encounter with the Logos of the hypostatic created Sophia who is manifested as the soul of the world, the queen of creation, the queen of heaven and earth.[5] In Mary and by her, he writes elsewhere, the feminine receives a place in spiritual devotion, in relation to the Holy Spirit. Making it clear that she is not the incarnation of the Holy Spirit, he affirms that Mary, 'the handmaid of the Lord', is a personality transparent to the action of the Holy Spirit.[6] Sophiology, it will readily be seen, has close links with mariology.

It is easy enough to perceive that Sophian doctrine has the effect of elevating womanhood to a major cosmic role. Indeed, for Solovyov, the universe, God's other, has from all eternity the image of perfect femininity, an image that can and should be realized and embodied in every living person. The eternal feminine is a living spiritual being, Sophia, possessing all the fullness of energies and activities, striving for this realization and embodiment in every person. The whole cosmic and historical process is for Solovyov a process of the realization and embodiment of this feminine principle in all sorts of forms and degrees.[7] For Evdokimov, a contemporary Russian theologian strongly marked by Jung, as well as by traditional Orthodox thought, the religious principle in mankind is expressed through woman, through the *anima*.[8] According to him, the Bible itself proclaims woman as the religious principle of human nature, the *fiat* of Mary at the annunciation being in close relationship with the creative *fiat* of God. To the divine paternity giving birth to the Son there corresponds the feminine maternity of Mary as the specific religious quality of human nature, a notion we also find in Claudel.[9] Man had no share in the Incarnation as a male element, only woman was involved, through Mary.[10] Contrary to popular misconception, woman is the stronger sex. Eve was tempted by Satan because she represented the religious principle in human life, it was that principle which Satan was at pains to corrupt; Adam merely followed Eve.[11] In the view of these sophiologists all creation in the human sphere is Sophian. Through the feminine principle of Sophia, writes Evdokimov, the awesome figure of Yahveh is transformed into a human face. The Virgin gives birth to Yahveh-man. Mary is the organ of Sophia.[12] Thus it can be seen that there is the most intimate connection between the Holy Spirit, Sophia, Mary and the feminine in itself, a connection which Evdokimov expressly makes, though taking care to point out that these expressions do not touch the essence of God, introduce no feminine element into the Godhead.[13] Sophia is also identified by Solovyov with the soul of the world and with Christ's Body, which in its universal aspect is the Church.[14] Sophian analogies are indeed almost limitless, as Sophia is in a sense the creative force itself. Apart from the distinction between uncreated Wisdom and creaturely Wisdom, which latter receives its perfect manifestation in Mary, a distinction that Bulgakov makes clear, it is sufficient to bear in mind, however, the general elevation and religious significance of womanhood that Sophian doctrine entails, and the particular associations it makes between the Holy Spirit, Sophia, Mary and the Church,[15] since Claudel himself regarded certain of these analogies, in particular Divine Wisdom, Mary and the Church, to which he added the human soul, as inherent in the meaning to be attached to woman generally throughout his work.[16]

It will no doubt have been noticed that the dual form of Sophia, the heavenly Sophia and the earthly Sophia, reflects a common division of celestial archetype and earthly embodiment.

The two Matronas or Shekinahs of Cabbalistic thought and the Neo-Platonic notion of a heavenly Venus and an earthly Venus express similar conceptions and similar distinctions. Indeed, the Shekinah of Cabbalistic thought is the Glory of God, an attribute deriving from the Book of Wisdom 7:25 and which Bulgakov expressly affirms.[17] It is of interest in passing to note that in the *Zohar* the Shekinah represents the feminine principle which comes forth from God but remains part of the divine world. God unites with the Shekinah who is also his daughter. The creation of the world, even according to the *Talmud*, is an act of divine fecundation and, still according to the *Talmud*, the Glory of God is present wherever a man and a woman unite in love.[18] Again according to the *Zohar*, man created in the image of God is man created in his double nature, male and female, a complementary dualism which runs through the whole of creation, reflecting in this way the divine nature.[19] Indeed, analogies are established in the *Zohar* between God, the spirit, the masculine, the light, on the one hand, and the universe, matter, the feminine, darkness, on the other.[20] Sophia, it may finally be observed, even has a place in gnostic cosmology where it fulfils a creative function analogous to that of biblical Wisdom. Sophia is even identified with Helen, said to be a converted prostitute, the companion of Simon the Magician, and who was known as the Mother of All.[21] In gnosticism, too, then, there seems to exist the idea of two Sophias, the divine and the earthly. It would appear from this brief excursion outside Christian thought that Sophian doctrine, as developed in Orthodox Christianity, is no isolated current of cosmological speculation, but does indeed follow what one may call the established pattern of such speculation, though it is obviously freed from the materialistic implications that Cabbalistic thinking could be interpreted as having. Indeed, one may easily understand, in the light of Cabbalistic cosmology, the need for the Orthodox sophiologist to make a distinction between the essence of God and the divine energies, even though this distinction itself remains a distinction-identity, since the unity of the Godhead must necessarily be preserved.[22]

We know, without any doubt, that for Claudel, as for sophiologists themselves, Divine Wisdom derives from the feminine
figure in the Book of Proverbs. He made this discovery on the
day of his conversion, 25 December 1886, opening his sister's
Protestant Bible and coming across the verses from Proverbs 8
that he later found to be used for the epistle at Mass on the feast of
the Immaculate Conception. Since these verses are germane to
the whole issue we are discussing, it is perhaps not inappropriate
to reproduce them:

> The Lord possessed me in the beginning of his way,
> Before his works of old.
> I was set up from everlasting, from the beginning,
> Or ever the earth was.
> When there were no depths, I was brought forth;
> When there were no fountains abounding with water.
> Before the mountains were settled,
> Before the hills was I brought forth:
> While as yet he had not made the earth, nor the fields,
> Nor the beginning of the dust of the world.
> When he established the heavens, I was there:
> When he set a circle upon the face of the deep:
> When he made firm the skies above:
> When the fountains of the deep became strong:
> When he gave to the sea its bound,
> That the waters should not transgress his commandment:
> When he marked out the foundations of the earth.
> Then I was by him, as a master workman:
> And I was daily his delight,
> Rejoicing always before him;
> Rejoicing in his habitable earth;
> And my delight was with the sons of men,
> Now therefore, my sons, hearken unto me:
> For blessed are they that keep my ways.
> Hear instruction and be wise,
> And refuse it not.

Blessed is the man that heareth me,
Watching daily at my gates,
Waiting at the posts of my doors,
For whoso findeth me findeth life,
And shall obtain favour of the LORD.

(Proverbs (RV) 9: 22–35)

Writing in 1955, the poet informs us that it was not long before he recognized in this 'radiant figure' the features of the Mother of God, 'en même temps qu'inséparables ceux de l'Eglise et de la Sagesse créée',[23] from which it seems that he then distinguished clearly enough between uncreated and created Wisdom. In case it should be thought that the octogenerian writer, primarily concerned as he was in his old age with biblical exegesis, should have reinterpreted his youthful concerns in the light of his later preoccupations, a letter of 1891, addressed to Mockel, makes it clear that the Princess, in *Tête d'or*, represents the human soul, woman, Wisdom and pity.[24] We also know that Marthe, in the first version of *L'Échange*, is, in the words of Claudel, writing to Jean-Louis Barrault in 1951, 'l'incarnation de cette créature mystérieuse du chapitre VIII des *Proverbes* (telle que je la réalisais alors) dont on trouvera le reflet dans toutes mes figures de femmes'.[25] Lâla, in the second version of *La Ville*, likewise partakes of Divine Wisdom, according to Claudel's broadcast talks with Jean Amrouche in 1951, as well as representing Grace.[26]

Though, in *J'aime la Bible*, Claudel claims that he was not long in recognizing the Virgin Mary, as well as created Wisdom, in the feminine figure of Proverbs, the first evidence we find in his work of this identification seems to be in the poem 'Le chant de marche de Noël', first published in March 1913, and included in *Corona benignitatis anni Dei*. In this poem, Mary is greeted with these words deriving from Proverbs 8:

Salut, femme à genoux dans la splendeur, première-née entre toutes les créatures!
Les abîmes n'étaient pas encore et déjà vous étiez conçue.

C'est vous qui avez fait que dans les cieux la lumière indéficiente est issue!

Quand il faisait une croix sur l'abîme, le Tout-puissant avait placé devant lui votre figure.

Comme je l'ai devant moi dans mon cœur, o grande fleur-de-lys, Vierge pure![27]

Claudel himself claimed in later life that his conversion to Catholicism was the work of the Virgin Mary.[28] In any case, the ode 'Magnificat' is deeply Marian and *L'Annonce faite à Marie*, composed between 1910 and 1911, develops Marian symbolism in more complex fashion. The identification of the creaturely Sophia with Mary, however, seems to have taken place in Claudel's mind some time in the years preceding 1913, but probably not long before that date. Gradually Mary assumes more and more importance in Claudel's thinking. Raymond Halter distinguishes three basic analogies with regard to Claudel's understanding of Divine Wisdom: Wisdom-Creation, with which aesthetic creation is inseparably linked;[29] Wisdom-Scripture, seen as God's reply to the anguish of the human heart; and Wisdom-Mary. This last-named became the dominant analogy, absorbing all the others:

La Vierge Marie, miroir le plus parfait qu'une créature fût jamais capable de présenter à la Sagesse incréée, en sorte que le Créateur l'ait prévue avec amour dès le commencement, devint progressivement pour le poète, la fin et le chef-d'œuvre de la Création, la mesure esthétique de son œuvre et la personnification de la Bible, sa réalisation vivante, donnée par Dieu à l'Humanité. De plus, le personnage de Marie jetait un pont entre l'événement survenu à Notre-Dame et la découverte consécutive de l'Écriture Sainte. Elle créait ainsi une profonde unité d'inspiration entre des éléments d'apparence divers, où le poète devait puiser jusqu'à la fin de sa vie[30]

In a poem of 1918, 'L'Architecte', included in *Feuilles des Saints*, Wisdom is not only identified with Mary in words taken from

Proverbs, but Mary is declared to be the source of all poetic inspiration, an example of the way in which for Claudel the creative function of Sophia, of which the poet partakes, becomes itself transferred to Mary:

> C'est elle [Mary] dont il est écrit que la première elle fut dans le dessein de Dieu;
> Et dont il portait l'image dans son cœur quand il fit avec son compas le premier cercle sur l'abîme!
> Et nous avant de rien faire, de même qui nous reprochera de regarder cette figure sublime?
> Notre œuvre quand nous y mettons la main, ce n'est pas là qu'elle s'éveille et commence,
> C'est quand, oubliant de penser à nous, pleins d'un respect profond et d'une admiration immense,
> Nous regardons ce Visage aimé où nous savons que jamais il n'y aura de colère pour nous.
> Vous qui êtes entre toutes les femmes la Femme, vous savez ce qu'est une femme pour nous![31]

Even though the Marian motif eventually dominates, this does not mean that the notion of Wisdom disappears from Claudel's later work. There are various references to Wisdom in his work,[32] as well as the two books of which Wisdom is the main theme, *La Sagesse ou le Parabole du Festin* (completed in 1935) and *Les Aventures de Sophie* (completed in 1936).

One of the most curious points of contact between Claudel's mariology and Russian sophiology is to be found in a passage from *La Liturgie, l'Eglise, la Sainte Vierge*, where the French poet expressly states that there are two Marys, a heavenly and an earthly Mary:

> Mais l'Eglise, dans le vocabulaire de la foi, c'est aussi la Sainte Vierge, c'est aussi Marie, et d'un bout à l'autre de l'Ecriture, il y a entre ces deux créatures communication de personnalités et de fonctions. L'une ne cesse de livrer à l'autre ce Dieu que l'amour a rendu prisonnier: N'est ce pas elle que, depuis ce

commencement qu'Il a en Lui-même, Il ne peut se lasser de regarder? [An obvious allusion to Proverbs.] Ce que Marie accomplit maintenant dans le ciel, il faut qu'une autre Marie, issue d'elle et participant à elle, l'accomplisse sur la terre. L'une et l'autre Marie! pour quelle raison Dieu a-t-il eu le soin de l'une et de l'autre Marie? Il me semble qu'elle est double . . .[33]

Clearly, this other Mary deriving from the heavenly Mary and partaking of her is the Church, but it does seem in this passage as if Claudel were making of Mary, assumed into heaven, uncreated Wisdom, the divine Sophia. The feminine figure of Proverbs, uncreated Wisdom in sophiological speculation, seems to have become identified in Claudel's mind with Mary, so that for the Church, the Body of Christ, he finds it necessary to write of another Mary, an earthly Mary – the role that Mary herself properly fulfils in Orthodox sophiology – to act as a unifying analogy. The poet has, in fact, it seems to me, elevated Mary to the role of the divine Sophia, the creative principle. The identification has become complete.

The important issue for the student of Claudel is to determine to what extent, if any, the notion of Divine Wisdom, with its ultimate Marian identification in the mind of the poet, affects the role of woman in his plays, he himself having frequently asserted that all his heroines symbolize in some degree this theological belief.[34] In the first place, one must emphasize that the basic factor for Claudel the poet-playwright is the feminine figure of Proverbs, rather than any speculation concerning her exact function, even though his later years were largely concerned with biblical exegesis. The fact that a woman is depicted in Proverbs as the first manifested being, living before the existence of the world, working with God in his creative activity as he brings the universe into being, rejoicing in his presence – jouant in the French version, more evocative of a frolicsome femininity – and being his constant delight, this is the main factor for him. Womanhood, through the analogy adopted in Proverbs, is intimately associated with the Godhead, notably in creative activity. From this it may be argued, as Evdokimov argues, that the religious principle in humanity is represented by the feminine. The sensitivity peculiar to the purely spiritual, he writes, resides in the *anima* and it is the feminine soul which is the nearest to the sources of Genesis,[35] words that are almost echoed by Claudel in *Les Aventures de Sophie*, where he refers to

> cette entente profonde qui s'est établie entre [la femme] et [Dieu]; cette chair que par la faute elle a mise à la disposition de la Rédemption. Elle dont Adam a dit qu'elle était *la chair de sa chair*. Quoi de plus propre à faire souvenir Dieu que nous ne sommes que chair, un esprit qui va et ne revient jamais. Il va et la chair va avec lui, mais où va-t-elle sinon vers son auteur? A toi, dit le Ps 64, 3, viendra toute chair.[36]

The Jungian notion of *anima* which Evdokimov adopts is also used by Claudel for whom the *anima* is the human soul, which is for him symbolized by woman. Also in *Les Aventures de Sophie*, Claudel writes a eulogy of woman that puts her on exactly the same spiritual plane where Evdokimov places her:

> Dieu lui a conféré ce visage qui, si lointain et déformé qu'il soit, est une certaine image de Sa perfection. Il l'a rendue désirable. Il a placé en elle la fin et l'origine, il l'a faite dépositaire de Ses desseins et capable de rendre à l'homme ce sommeil créateur dans lequel elle-même a été conçue. Elle est le support de sa destinée. Elle est le don [an attribute, it may be said, which links her with Grace as well as with the Holy Spirit]. Elle est la possibilité de la possession. Elle est ce qui à notre endroit est susceptible d'affection et d'interêt. Elle est l'attache de ce lien affectueux qui ne cesse d'unir le créateur à Son œuvre. Elle le comprend. Elle est l'âme qui voit et qui fait. Elle partage avec Lui en quelque manière la patience et le pouvoir de la création.[37]

Claudel goes on to apply to woman verses taken from *The Song of Songs* which show the desire of woman that God himself has.

In the earlier plays it is quite apparent, only too apparent, that roles such as that of the Princess in *Tête d'or*, of Marthe in *L'Échange* and Lâla in *La Ville* are highly symbolic. As long ago as 1948 Pascal Ryswalski identified the first-named as a personification of Wisdom, having recognized in a speech of hers certain verses from Proverbs I.[38] The Sophian nature of Marthe and Lâla are less obvious, particuarly in the case of the former. With respect to Lâla, who also embodies the idea of Grace,[39] one may perhaps see something of the frolicsome nature of the feminine figure of Proverbs; Lâla also helps in an indirect way in the building of the new city, having been for a time the companion of Coeuvre, the priest-poet, and being the mother of Ivors, the leader of the new city. It is possible to see in this rather remote but essential contribution to the creation of the new city some reflection of the Sophian function, but it hardly seems likely that a reader unversed in sophiology and ignorant of Claudel's own intention, as expressed in 1951, would draw such a conclusion.

If we turn to the later plays, written after the encounter on the boat to China in 1901 had infused Claudel's idea of woman with a poignant living quality, a deeply felt emotion, notably in *Partage de midi*, it seems to me that the Sophian function of woman is not only more clearly perceptible but forms in fact one of the basic data, which it is the intention of the poet to demonstrate in certain plays. In *Le Soulier de satin*, in particular, we are presented with a demonstration of woman's soterial function, her Beatrician capacity to bring salvation to the man she loves and who loves her. It is Solovyov's view of Sophian activity, the realization of perfect femininity which is spiritual perfection, in each living creature, to which, it seems to me, Claudel comes nearest, it being the function of his major heroines, in however devious a manner, to bring their lovers to spiritual fruition, to create of them the children of God they were intended to be, to which end they have also to realize their own spiritual selves. Such activity is essentially Sophian.

In *Partage de midi* itself, the issue of man's love for woman and hers for him in an adulterous context is so intensely, burningly, felt that the mutual creation in one another of the child of God is hardly given much development. Indeed, in these circumstances the whole enterprise seems dauntingly hazardous. There is in any case less theology than lyricism in this play which undoubtedly benefits as a theatrical production from the theological discretion, even though Ysé's final volte-face seems to be dictated purely by the poet's desire for a spiritual denouement from which she is not excluded. That in itself, however, reflects a Sophian spirit. In this contradictory situation of love in adultery that *Partage de midi* portrays, Ysé has at one point the intuition that in all love the man and woman create one another in their full complementary development:

> O mon Mesa, tu n'es plus un homme seulement, mais tu es à moi qui suis une femme,
> Et je suis un homme en toi, et tu es une femme avec moi, et je cueille ton cœur sans que tu saches comment.
> Et je l'ai pris, et je l'arrange avec moi pour toujours entre mes deux seins![40]

In this same act, however, she also recognizes that adulterous love cannot be properly creative, but bears in it an element of destruction:

> Mais ce que nous désirons, ce n'est point de créer, mais de détruire . . .
> Non, ceci n'est pas un mariage
> Qui unit toute chose à l'autre, mais une rupture et le jurement mortel et la préférence de toi seul![41]

But, with his deeply religious understanding, Mesa realizes that love, though it may be forbidden in certain circumstances, is essentially creative:

> Et je te sens sous moi passionnément qui abjure, et en moi le profond dérangement
> De la création, comme la Terre,
> Lorsque l'écume aux lèvres elle produisait la chose aride, et que dans un rétrécissement effroyable
> Elle faisait sortir sa substance et le repli des monts comme de la pâte![42]

In the final reunion of these lovers, in the closing scene of Act III, reference is clearly made, in the original version of the play, which is the finest, to the creativeness of their love. Before Ysé returns, Mesa affirms that she has destroyed the whole world for him and nothing existed any longer but she herself; now by her withdrawal she is destroying him and he clings to God alone. But this is in fact only the preparation for the full development of Mesa ultimately achieved in the accepted love of Ysé, for, when she returns, he asks her:

> Dis, est-ce que tu m'entends à présent? est-ce que tu sens vivre
> Mon souffle au fond de tes entrailles? est ce que tu es sous ma parole comme quelqu'un de créé? Ah, sois ma vie, mon Ysé, et sois mon âme, et ma vie, et sois mon cœur, et dans mes bras le soulèvement de celui qui naît! [43]

This is indeed the Sophian creativity of love. Ysé is no longer the old Ysé. To borrow her own words, she now sees everything and is herself wholly seen, 'et il n'y a qu'amour en nous, Nets et nus, faisant l'un de l'autre vie, dans une interpénétration Inexprimable...' [44] In this work, the dramatic emphasis lies less on Sophian creativity than on the ardent feeling of two people who love one another with passionate intensity, but the intention of the final act, however dubious the actual working out may seem to the theologically critical, is fully Sophian.

This same intention underlies *Le Soulier de satin*, where it is the function of Prouhèze to become the child of God, the perfection of womanhood in the person of Prouhèze, so that she may lead Rodrigue to the same self-realization. And it is her love of him which leads her to seek this spiritual fulfilment. In this play Sophian creativity may seem at first sight more obscured even than in *Partage de midi*, where the lovers do ultimately fulfil themselves as children of God in the full acceptance of one another, however unprepared the reader or spectator may feel for this spiritual transfiguration of hero and heroine. In *Le Soulier de satin* they quite clearly renounce one another, so that the pain of separation and renunciation plays a major part in the working out of their destinies. After being a cross on which Rodrigue is nailed,[45] Prouhèze becomes his guiding star in heaven.[46] Nevertheless, the basic thought is Sophian. The words of Prouhèze in the Second Day, Scene XIV, make it clear that she understands that she is to give birth to the essential Rodrigue, the fully realized child of God,

> Comme Adam, quand il dormit, la première femme.
>
> Quand je le tiendrai ainsi par tous les bouts de son corps et par toute la texture de sa chair et de sa personne par le moyen de ces clous en moi profondément enfoncés,
>
> Quand il n'y aura plus aucun moyen de s'échapper, quand il sera fixé à moi pour toujours dans cet impossible hymen, quand il n'y aura plus moyen de s'arracher à ce cric de ma chair puissante et à ce vide impitoyable, quand je lui aurai prouvé son néant avec le mien, quand il n'y aura plus dans son néant de secret que le mien ne soit capable de vérifier,
>
> C'est alors que je le donnerai à Dieu découvert et déchirée pour qu'il le remplisse dans un coup de tonnerre, c'est alors que j'aurai un époux et que je tiendrai un dieu entre mes bras !
>
> Mon Dieu, je verrai sa joie ! je le verrai avec vous et c'est moi qui en serai la cause !
>
> Il a demandé Dieu à une femme et elle était capable de le lui donner, car il n'y a rien au ciel et sur la terre que l'amour ne soit capable de donner ![47]

The words of the Guardian Angel, in the Third Day, Scene VIII, imply that in the very love for one another that Prouhèze and Rodrigue have there is a creative force, an intimate association in the mystery of God's creation, in the activity of Sophia. He asks Prouhèze:

> Est-ce l'oublier que d'être avec Lui? est-ce ailleurs qu'avec Lui d'être associé au mystère de Sa création,
>
> Franchissant de nouveau pour un instant l'Eden par la porte de l'humiliation et de la mort?[48]

In this same scene the role of woman as such is stressed by the aesthetically embarrassing Guardian Angel:

> Pour les uns l'intelligence suffit. C'est l'esprit qui parle purement à l'esprit.
>
> Mais pour les autres il faut que la chair aussi peu à peu soit évangelisée et convertie. Et quelle chair pour parler à l'homme plus puissante que celle de la femme?
>
> Maintenant il ne pourra plus te désirer sans désirer en même temps où tu es.[49]

Prouhèze fully understands, at least after the theological explanation offered by her Guardian Angel, God's close association with woman through the Incarnation which brings her into union with God, for she explains this relationship to Camille:

> Ce qui a été cloué sur la croix n'était pas un déguisement.
>
> Cette union qu'Il a contractée avec la femme était vraie, ce néant qu'Il est allé rechercher jusque dans le sein de la femme.[50]

With Camille also, Prouhèze has a relationship of Sophian creativity, creating of him, however reluctantly, by the person she is and by the spiritually perfected person she becomes, the essential Camille. His call to her: 'Ah! cessez d'être une femme et laissez-moi voir sur votre visage enfin ce Dieu que vous êtes impuissante à contenir Et atteindre au fond de votre cœur cette eau dont Dieu vous a faite le vase',[51] is answered by the radiance he sees in her countenance.

In the final meeting between Rodrigue and Prouhèze, it is made quite clear that she has become one with God, perfect womanhood expressed in the person of Prouhèze:

> Ce que veut Celui qui me possède c'est cela seulement que je veux, ce que veut Celui-là en qui je suis anéantie c'est en cela que tu as à faire de me retrouver!
>
> N'accuse que toi-même, Rodrigue! ce qu'aucune femme n'était capable de fournir pourquoi me l'avoir demandé?
>
> Pourquoi avoir fixé sur mon âme ces deux yeux dévorateurs?

ce qu'ils me demandaient j'ai essayé de l'avoir pour te le donner!

Et maintenant pourquoi m'en vouloir parce que je ne sais plus promettre mais seulement donner et que la vision et le don ne font plus avec moi que cet unique éclair?

. . . .

Je veux être avec toi dans le principe! Je veux épouser ta cause! je veux apprendre avec Dieu à ne rien réserver, à être cette chose toute bonne et toute donnée qui ne réserve rien et à qui l'on prend tout!

Prends, Rodrigue, prends, mon cœur, prends, mon amour, prends ce Dieu qui me remplit!

La force par laquelle je t'aime n'est pas différente de celle par laquelle tu existes.

Je suis unie pour toujours à cette chose qui te donne la vie éternelle!

Le sang n'est pas plus uni à la chair que Dieu ne me fait sentir chaque battement de ce cœur dans ta poitrine qui à chaque seconde de la bienheureuse éternité

S'unit et se résépare.[52]

The union of the two lovers and the union of the woman with God could hardly be expressed with less ambiguity. Woman is, in this play, to use Evdokimov's expression, the religious principle in mankind, even if Prouhèze has a hard path to follow to achieve the realization of this principle in herself. Prouhèze and Rodrigue do create of one another by their love, despite the adulterous context, despite the pain of separation and seeming betrayal, the completely realized spiritual being that fulfils God's purpose. The words of Prouhèze in the shortened stage version of the play are even more clearly Sophian than in the original version, for she there says: 'Mais Rodrigue a créé un monde et c'est moi qui ai créé Rodrigue.' [53] In the man, in Rodrigue, we see but the first stage of this realization, the privation, the humiliation, but in the woman we see the perfect realization, for woman in Claudel's thinking, as in Evdokimov's, is by her nature as woman closer to God, being through Mary the instrument of salvation, an instrumentality that devolves potentially on all women. Prouhèze gives spiritual birth to the essential Rodrigue, thus sharing in Sophian creativity, as Mary herself does, being, to use the terminology of Bulgakov, the perfect image of created Wisdom. In the figure of Musique in *Le Soulier de satin*, that lighthearted woman full of love and joyousness, the expression of self-offering in love, we may also see a reflection of the woman of Proverbs, a reminder of perfect love realized in confidence and serenity. It is the aim of this essay, not only to attempt a short elucidation of the meaning of Sophia in Claudel's work, but also to suggest briefly that Claudel's claim that woman represents Wisdom, among other analogies, in all his feminine portrayals is not perhaps unjustified.

NOTES

1. C. G. Jung, *Collected Works*, Vol. 11, London: Routledge, 1958, pp. 386–7.
2. St Gregory Palamas, quoted by Olivier Clément, *Byzance et le Christianisme*. Paris: Presses Universitaires de France, 1964, p. 78.
3. ibid., p. 78. Proverbs (RV), 9 : 1 reads: 'Wisdom hath builded her house, She hath hewn out her seven pillars.'
4. See N. O. Lossky, *History of Russian Philosophy*, London: Allen and Unwin, 1952, pp. 206 ff.
5. Serge Boulgakof, *Du Verbe incarné (Agnus Dei)*, traduit du russe par Constantin Andronikof, Paris: Aubier, 1943, pp. 129–31.
6. Sergius Bulgakov, *The Orthodox Church*, London: The Centenary Press, 1935, p. 140.
7. See N. O. Lossky, op. cit., pp. 103–4.
8. Paul Evdokimov, *La Femme et le Salut du Monde, Etude d'Anthropologie chrétienne sur les charismes de la femme*, Tournai: Casterman, 1958, p. 148.
9. Paul Claudel, *J'aime la Bible*, Paris; Fayard, 1955, p. 107.
10. Paul Evdokimov, op. cit., p. 152.
11. ibid., pp. 153–4.
12. ibid., pp. 198–9.
13. ibid., p. 215.
14. See N. O. Lossky, op. cit., p. 104.
15. C. G. Jung indicates the association between Mary, Sophia and the Holy Spirit in the *Answer to Job*, op. cit., p. 407.
16. Paul Claudel, *Mémoires improvisés*, Paris, Gallimard, 1954, p. 51.
17. *Du Verbe incarné*, p. 29. Wisdom, 7: 25–6 (Knox), reads: 'Steam that ascends from the fervour of divine activity, pure effluence of his glory who

is God all-powerful, she feels no passing taint; she, the glow that mediates from eternal light, she, the untarnished mirror of God's majesty, she, the fulfilled echo of his goodness.'

18. S. Karppe, *Étude sur les origines et la nature du Zohar*, Paris: Alcan, 1901, pp. 64, 426.

19. ibid., p. 457. According to the *Zohar* (III, 44b), man and woman were originally one being whom God subsequently separated into two.

20. ibid., pp. 427, 430.

21. See R. M. Grant, *Gnosticism and Early Christianity*, New York: Columbia University Press, London: O.U.P., 1959, pp. 76 ff.

22. See Olivier Clément, op. cit., pp. 39 ff, and Vladimir Lossky, *The Mystical Theology of the Eastern Church*, London: Clarke, 1957, esp. ch. IV, 'Uncreated Energies,' pp. 67 ff.

23. *J'aime la Bible*, p. 8.

24. Paul Claudel, *Œuvres Complètes*, VI, Paris: Gallimard, 1953, p. 409.

25. Paul Claudel, *Œuvres Complètes*, VIII, 1954, p. 394.

26. Paul Claudel, *Mémoires improvisés*, pp. 90-1.

27. Paul Claudel, *Œuvres Complètes*, I, 1950, p. 360. Quoted in part by Raymond Halter, *La Vierge Marie dans la vie et l'oeuvre de Paul Claudel*, Paris: Mame, 1958, pp. 55-6.

28. Paul Claudel, *Œuvres Complètes*, II, 1952, p. 303. 'C'est tout de même vous, Madame (Marie) qui avez eu l'initiative', the first line of the poem: 'Le 25 Décembre 1886'. The poem was completed on 8 September 1942.

29. In a letter to Gide, of 7.11.1905, Claudel wrote: 'Ne voyez-vous pas le principe d'un art éclatant et généreux dans le chapitre des Proverbes où l'on voit la Sagesse "jouant" sur l'abîme dans une liberté sublime?' *Paul Claudel et André Gidé. Correspondance*, 1899-1926, Paris: Gallimard, 1949, p. 52. Quoted by Raymond Halter, op. cit., pp. 27-8.

30. Raymond Halter, op. cit., p. 18.

31. Paul Claudel, *Œuvres Complètes*, II, p. 94. Quoted by Raymond Halter, op. cit., p. 59. I am much indebted to this work, which is insufficiently known, for the quotations from *Le Chant de Marche de Noël*, *L'Architecte*, and the Gide-Claudel correspondence.

32. e.g. at the end of the poem on Dante, (*O.C. II*, p. 181); at the end of an essay on Homer (Pl. IV, p. 410); in an essay on Aeschylus, (Pl.IV,p.420). In both of these latter two, Wisdom is linked with the Greek notion of Athene. In a note to an essay on Hugo (Pl. IV, p. 467), Wisdom is even linked with Cassandra and Phaedra.

33. Paul Claudel, *Œuvres Complètes*, XXV, 1965, p. 542.

34. e.g. *Mémoires improvisés*, p. 91; the letter to Jean-Louis Barrault of 17.6.1951 *Œuvres Complètes*, VIII, p. 394; *J'aime la Bible*, p. 8.

35. Paul Evdokimov, *La Femme et le Salut du Monde*, p. 148.

36. Paul Claudel, *Œuvres Complètes*, *XIX*, 1962, p. 36.
37. Paul Claudel, *Œuvres Complètes*, *XIX*, p. 37.
38. Pascal Ryswalski, *Claudel et la Bible*, Porrentruy: Editions des Portes de France, 1948, pp. 78–9.
39. Paul Claudel, *Mémoires improvisés*, p. 91.
40. Paul Claudel, *Œuvres Complètes*, *XI*, 1957, p. 62. I quote only from the original version which is for me the most satisfactory.
41. ibid., pp. 66–8.
42. ibid., p. 67.
43. ibid., p. 96.
44. ibid., p. 103.
45. Paul Claudel, *Œuvres Complètes*, *XII*, 1958, pp. 144, 217. Except where otherwise stated, I quote from the original version of the play.
46. ibid., pp. 192, 235.
47. ibid., p. 145.
48. ibid., p. 190.
49. ibid., p. 193.
50. ibid., p. 216.
51. ibid., p. 218.
52. ibid., pp. 234–6.
53. ibid., p. 510.

8 · '. . . la prosodie me fut enseignée par les psaumes. . .' Some reflections on Claudel's *verset*

ELFRIEDA DUBOIS

LOOKING BACK on his earliest impressions Claudel recalls: 'C'est au son des cloches et à la mélopée des vêpres que j'ai puisé le sens de cette prosodie empruntée aux psaumes qui exaspère tellement les tenants de notre bel alexandrin.'[1] Some ten years later, on the occasion of a gala performance of *L'Annonce faite à Marie*, Claudel evoked his native village and the countryside around which represents 'le pays de l'Annonce'. 'C'est là où la prosodie me fut enseignée, et ce n'est aucun *Dictionnaire des rimes* que j'eus besoin d'acheter, mais la grande voix catholique des psaumes, ce grand psaume 113 des Vêpres en particulier, *In Exitu Israel de Egypto*, qui m'emportait comme une Marseillaise.'[2] This prosody corresponded to his natural poetic gift as he recollected in the last years of his life: '. . . dès que j'ai eu treize ou quatorze ans, je me suis trouvé une vocation d'écrivain, de poète. Je me rappelle des poèmes que j'écrivais à quatorze ans, qui étaient déjà faits dans le rythme prosodique que j'ai adopté plus tard, qui m'est entièrement naturel.'[3] After this first, mainly aural, impression of the Bible came the years of adolescent unbelief. Then, on the evening of Christmas Day 1886, returning home from Notre-Dame, Claudel opened the Bible, in the Ostervald translation, given to him by his sister Camille.

> C'est le jour même de ma conversion . . . que je la rencontrai [la Sagesse]. Ce jour-là, pour ne plus la refermer, j'ouvris la Bible à deux endroits: le premier, c'était la rencontre d'Emmaüs. Le second, c'était le chapitre VIII des Proverbes . . .[4]

But he came to the Latin text at an early date through the use of the missal and the reading of the breviary. This was certainly a well established habit by 1908; he wrote to Suarès '. . . mon Bréviaire que je lis tous les jours . . .' [5] Claudel was consciously aware of the rhythm of the psalms, and of other parts of the Old Testament, whilst composing his *Cinq grandes odes*[6] where he was to work out his own form of poetic expression. He explained to Rivière that 'Je compose en ce moment la dernière des quatre *Grandes Odes* ou *psaumes* ou monologues . . .'[7] and later, acknowledging Rivière's critical study of his poetry, he admitted an almost unconscious feeling of frustration at his inability to use the traditional metre: 'Calmerez-vous ainsi le vieux remords que je sens à n'avoir pas su me servir du vers canonique?' [8] He felt ill at ease in any 'forme extérieurement imposée'.[9] He envisaged his poetry as a dialogue with the perceptive and sympathetic reader: '. . . mon vers n'est jamais qu'un cri, une *proposition* dans la solitude, qui ne se passe pour exister de la foi et de l'acceptation d'un auditeur ami'.[10] The at once emotional (*cri*) and intellectual (*proposition*) character of his poetry as well as the implied dialogue has an analogy in the psalms.

Questioned on the poetic influences he had experienced, he stressed his indebtedness to the prosody of the psalms. In reply to criticism of the irregularities of his style and the boldness of his composition, ascribed to the influence of Pindar, Claudel explained:

> Il y a un auteur que j'ai encore beaucoup plus fréquenté puisque je le lis à peu près tous les jours, c'est celui des Psaumes. Tous les reproches que vous m'adressez, incohérence dans les idées, désordre, violences grammaticales, obscurité, pourraient aussi bien et davantage s'adresser à lui . . .[11]

In order to defend his own free use of syntax and prosody, Claudel pointed to the irregularities of Jerome's Latin, welcoming its freedom:

> La correction que les Anges t'ont administrée, il faut croire que c'était pour de bon !
>
> Jérôme, je les remercie à coups de fouet pour toujours qui t'ont exorcisé de Cicéron !

Later in the same poem he explains that

> L'important est de sortir du ventre d'Abraham, et de sortir
> Isaïe et David, et de sortir l'Ecclésiaste et les Psaumes! . . . et
> tant pis pour Quintilien . . .[12]

Claudel followed both the rhythmical and the structural pattern
of the psalms with which he was, however, familiar through
translations only. Ostervald's rendering in the first instance, close
to the original, but unimaginative and disregarding the Hebrew
rhythm. In his article on the new, so called Jerusalem version
of the psalms,[13] Schwab points to 'Le style factice dont la lourdeur,
la lenteur, sont devenues abusivement inséparables de la lecture
biblique . . .'

Claudel's earliest memories were of the Latin text of the Bible
(accompanied by plainchant) and to this he returned. Any French
translation became distasteful to him: 'Toutes les traductions
françaises me font mal au cœur . . .'[14] In fact the reading of one
such, the Crampon translation, filled him with admiration for the
Vulgate text: 'C'est en lisant la traduction de Crampon qu'on est
pénétré d'admiration pour la *Vulgate* et St Jérôme . . .'[15] Reflecting on his scriptural readings towards the end of his life he stressed
the poetic quality of the Vulgate:

> Nous avons le bonheur de posséder dans la Vulgate une
> traduction des Livres Saints qui est un monument poétique, que
> je ne suis pas loin de considérer personnellement comme le chef
> d'œuvre de la langue latine. S'il n'est pas inspiré au sens
> théologique, il est certainement *inspiré* au sens littéraire, comme
> on dit que l'*Iliade* et l'*Enéide* sont des œuvres inspirées.[16]

Had he not here found the justification for his vocation as a writer
that had caused hm so many misgivings earlier in life? 'Je ne suis
qu'un poète. Mais après tout qu'est-ce qu'est la Bible sinon un
immense poème?'[17]

Awakened to the understanding and writing of poetry during
the experimental turmoil of the later eighteen eighties, Claudel
made two discoveries: Rimbaud 'La lecture des *Illuminations*,

puis, quelques mois après, d'*Une Saison en enfer*, fut pour moi un
événement capital . . .'[18] – and Mallarmé 'qui était tout le passé fut
aussi l'avenir . . .'[19] for 'l'aventure d'Igitur est terminée et avec
la sienne celle de tout le dix-neuvième siècle.'[20] He was conscious
of arriving on the poetic scene at the time of a major break in the
poetic tradition: 'Il y a eu en France deux périodes de poésie
classique. La première, qui comprend le dix-septième siècle, la
seconde, qui va de Leconte de Lisle à Mallarmé et qui s'achève
sous nos yeux.'[21] Claudel began by rebelling against the most
established form of French verse: 'les malherbiens à la mécan-
ique'.[22] He wished poetry once and for all to be rid of that
'abominable métronome dont le battement de tournebroche
couvre notre jeu et de la voix de cette vieille maîtresse de piano
qui ne cesse de hurler à notre coude: un – deux – trois – quatre –
cinq – six!'[23] Claudel linked the rigid pattern of the alexandrine
to a general propensity in the French character towards a rigid
system of behaviour. But the alexandrine is also 'le vers d'un
peuple qui sait compter.'[24] With the alexandrine goes the
regular rhyme pattern, so detrimental to the freedom and range
of expression: '. . . l'obligation de rimer et de rimer bien rejette
le poète soit sur des associations de sons banales et éprouvées, soit
sur des sonorités les plus communes . . .'[25] But Claudel's attitude
to traditional French verse remained complex. He preferred
Boileau's terseness 'la forme stricte de l'alexandrin lui confère les
caractères de la nécessité et de l'évidence'; his 'lignes indestruc-
tibles' to Victor Hugo's 'padding', *la cheville*, so frequent in his
verses 'dont l'auteur bouche mal les interstices avec tout ce qui
lui tombe sous la main de bien voyant . . .'[26] At the end of his
life, although firm in his dislike of the traditional metre

> Niez l'ennui insoutenable, niez la monotonie de ces homo-
> phonies et de ces alternances que je compare, si douloureuses
> pour l'œil et pour l'attention, à celle des vides et des pleins dans
> une palissade interminable . . .'[27]

and reminded by his fictitious interlocutor Arcas that at one time
he had 'si vertement critiqué l'alexandrin pour l'usage dramatique',

he nevertheless conceded that it was admirably suited to Racine's dramatic genius. 'Je ne l'admets pas seulement, j'y applaudis . . . C'était l'engin adéquat dont il avait besoin . . .' [28] In the Radio Interviews of 1951–2 he admitted that 'toutes les formes de vers sont absolutment justifiables, à condition qu'elles répondent à un besoin d'expression,' [29] even though he found the 'énumération de douze pieds . . . monstrueuse' [30]. The classical *distique* '. . . c'est sur ce couple alterné d'une proposition et d'une réponse que reposait jusqu'à ces derniers temps la prosodie française . . .' [31] was followed, according to Claudel, by a prosody based on 'la phrase et le motif', introduced by the romantic revolution. The motif 'impose sa forme et son impulsion à tout son poème.' [32] From the examples quoted (the regular repetition of 'Maintenant que' at the beginning of lines in *A Villequier*) it would seem that Claudel saw there a pattern of parallelism he adopted himself and which has an analogy in Hebrew poetry. Only through the adoption of the *vers libre* could really new rhythms be introduced into French poetry.

Claudel's approach to prosody was always closely linked to his general philosophical considerations: 'J'ajoute que ces deux théories par lesquelles je justifie la forme instructive de vers que j'ai inventée – théorie de la respiration – théorie de la différence – servent aussi de base à ma philosophie.' [33] In one of his earliest definitions he combined the two elements of his prosody, the intellectual and the rhythmic or musical: 'J'appelle vers l'haleine intelligible; le membre logique, l'unité sonore constituée par l'iambe ou rapport abstrait du grave et de l'aigu.' [34] This physiological basis of the metre was clear to him at the time of writing *Tête d'or*. In the same letter to Mockel he spoke of 'deux souffles: la poitrine et l'inspiration'. This inner rhythm – 'J'entends mon cœur en moi et l'horloge au centre de la maison' [35] – is related to our experience of time. 'Le mètre que l'âme constitue', the rhythm created by heart beat and breathing, corresponds to 'l'iambe fondamental en rapport d'une grave et d'une aigue' [36] when it is transposed into verse. Thought too follows a rhythmical pattern similar to the basic natural pattern: 'La pensée bat comme la cervelle et le cœur'. [37] If Claudel rejected the mere arithmetical counting in the traditional metre he substituted for it, by a slight semantic twist, another manner of 'counting', *le cœur qui compte*. 'De tout ce que l'esprit par le moyen des sens apprend, le cœur *prend compte*.' [38] Any change in the world outside us that we experience corresponds to a modification in our consciousness. This interrelation between *conscience* and *connaissance*[39] is transposed in the verse line

> La connaissance se transforme en conscience, l'impression en expression, le motif en émotion, la sensation intelligente en un rythme . . . Il [le coeur] demande à l'esprit de quoi alimenter ce branle, cette phrase de désir, de douleur et de contemplation qu'il a entreprise, et à qui en un mètre accéléré ou ralenti, il fournit impulsion, résilience, ictus. C'est ainsi que dans la voix . . . des vrais poètes on sent battre un coeur dont le *temps* se communique au nôtre.[40]

Claudel came to the iambic metre from different angles. He found it in Greek drama, in particular through his translation of the *Oresteia*. He had learnt from it that

> le vers dramatique, tel qu'il a été pratiqué par tous les maîtres antiques et par Shakespeare lui-même, n'est pas . . . le vers narratif, hexamètre ou alexandrin, rimé ou non. Le mètre scénique essentiel est l'iambe ou l'assemblage d'une brève et d'une longue auquel contre l'idée courante je maintiens que notre langue est plus qu'aucune autre adaptée . . .[41]

His perceptive judgment as to the suitability of the iambic metre to French has been confirmed by the scholars who translated the psalms from the original text: 'L'accent affectant le plus souvent la fin du mot hébreu, le rythme est ascendant ou anacrousique, comme celui du français: il est donc possible de rendre assez exactement en cette langue moderne les iambes ou les anapestes de l'hébreu.' [42] One could therefore claim a double source for the *verset*, one observed in the rhythm of tne psalms, the other closely studied in Greek drama. To this one must add the rhythm of every day conversation: 'Quel dialogue entre ces voix ... quel tour toujours nouveau! Quelles coupes! Quels rapports plus délicieux entre les timbres que ceux du rouge et du gris ...' [43] What Claudel puts in place of the counting of syllables is the 'accord entre une dominante choisie à un point variable de la phrase et la cadence finale.' [44] This stress on the final cadence of the verse line, so important to Claudel, has a parallel in plain-chant where the final cadence of each verse is also based on the last or last two tonic accents. Claudel anticipated any accusation directed at the *verset* as being mere prose, by stressing not only the visual aspect of the line 'le vers est une idée isolée par le blanc' [45] but also the aural, musical aspect:

> ... les différences de distance et de hauteur qui séparent les sommets phonétiques suffisent à créer pour chaque phrase un dessin sensible à notre œil auditif en même temps que le jeu des consonnes et de la syntaxe associé à celui des timbres indique la tension et le mouvement de l'idée.[46]

Prose could however contain a rhythm more valid than the one found in poetry. 'Les grands *poètes français* ... s'appellent Rabelais, Pascal, Bossuet, Saint-Simon, Chateaubriand, Honoré de Balzac, Michelet ...' [47] In Pascal, in particular, he found '... les principes de la phrase iambique ou anapestique qui a servi plus tard de base à mon art, et qu'on trouve également dans Bossuet ...' [48] He found the *vers libre* [49] congenial since it is 'soumis à des règles prosodiques extrêmement souples, c'est le vers des Psaumes et des Prophètes, celui de Pindare et des chœurs grecs, et aussi, somme toute le vers blanc de Shakespeare ...' [50]

The first suggestion of a *rapprochement* between the *verset* and the prosody of the psalms was made by Braunschwig: [51] 'C'est à la lecture de la Bible, dont il s'est nourri, qu'il a sans doute pris l'idée des versets dont il use dans ses poèmes lyriques et dans ses drames.' But this remained a general and isolated statement. Some years earlier, in the chapter devoted to prosody, J. Madaule[52] had pointed out the iambic basis of the Claudelian line and its justification in French.

In her *Introduction à Paul Claudel*, C. Chomez drew attention to the Biblical influences on Claudel's verse: 'C'est par centaines que l'on retrouverait dans ses poèmes les balancements et les parallélismes du style oral primitif... Le plus profond de sa mémoire verbale vibre aux mêmes cadences que David et Salomon.' [53] But she considered Claudel's thought too complex to fit into the rhythm of the psalms.

The first searching study of Claudel's prosody came from a musician. As such, J. Samson stressed Claudel's repeated insistence on the priority of the sound over the word. He gave serious thought to the *rapprochement* with Hebrew poetry, pointing to the various forms of parallelism: 'La lyrique claudélienne vit de ces procédés; elle y trouve les formes les mieux appropriées à ses besoins spécifiques d'expression.' [54] Quoting parallel passages of Biblical and Claudelian texts, J. Samson remarked that 'C'est du parallélisme de synonymie et de synthèse que Claudel use le plus'.[55] The units within the line as well as the stanza of the Claudelian verse show a clear similarity with the structure of the psalms.

Seemingly unaware of J. Samson's observations on the *verset*, P. Rywalski[56] in his chapter on prosody begins with Claudel's recollection of his first impression on hearing the psalms sung. While he concedes a certain resemblance of the Hebrew (or Vulgate) line and the *verset*, he denies, without any close investigation, the parallelism of Hebrew poetry in Claudel's prosody.

Of the three articles concerned with style and prosody in the obituary number of the *NRF*, the one based on l'*Histoire de Tobie et de Sara*[57] seems to contain the most fruitful suggestions. The author's first point concerns a certain similarity between Claudel's unorthodox, and Hebrew syntax. His second point deals with prosody and shows the use of parallelism, as in Biblical prosody – '... phrases sans charpente, mais non sans rythme, à l'imitation des poètes hébreux, Paul Claudel aime le parallélisme...' Claudel's use of the Bible, the author aptly concludes, was a creative one and by no means a mere imitation.

Taking as a starting point the line from 'Les Muses', 'Toute parole . . . une répétition,' G. Antoine[58] sees repetition as a basic feature of Claudel's poetry. His own discovery of this inner echo[59] induced him to draw a parallel with the rhythm of music and dance. G. Antoine rightly points to a 'dialogue de soi avec un autre soi-même' which is not absent from the Psalms. The analysis of the *Cinq grandes odes* on the principle of 'répétition' produces several forms of parallelism: 'de contradiction', 'de similitude', and borrowing a term from Biblical scholarship 'parallélisme de synthèse'.

In a later article [60] G. Antoine examines the syntactical structure of Claudel's verse and shows that the line contains semantic units which follow both meaning and musical rhythm. The frequent use of the syntactical ante-position (of the type 'Laisse-toi persuader par ces eaux peu à peu qui te délient', *Le Soulier de satin*) lends the line a flexible pattern of units. This would link up with the thematic analysis of A. Vachon and, allowing for the linguistic differences, with the word-thought unit of Hebrew poetry. A. Vachon traces some of Claudel's prosody to certain old liturgical hymns or sequences. Their influence is particularly marked in the *Processional* and in a number of pieces of the *Corona benignitatis anni Dei*. He also makes the very relevant distinction between *vers libre* and *verset*

> Mais il suffit de comparer les *Odes* avec n'importe quel recueil poétique de Régnier ou de Verhaeren, pour que la différence saute aux yeux: le vers de Claudel n'est jamais un mélange plus ou moins déguisé d'alexandrins, d'octo-syllabes et d'autres mètres réguliers; il ne rappelle en aucune manière la métrique traditionnelle . . .[61]

Conceding a first sight resemblance of the *verset* and the line of the psalter he leaves the question of a close resemblance open: 'Certes, les cas de parallélisme ne semblent pas fréquents chez Claudel, réserve faite des résultats, peut-être surprenants, qu'une analyse minutieuse des textes pourrait apporter'.[62]

Lastly comes Y. Scalzitti's analysis[63] of Claudel's metre showing the part played by stress 'rythme tonique' and the length of syllables 'rythme prosodique'. Although Claudel uses both, stress is preponderant, unlike in Saint-John Perse's *verset* which derives from it. The *verset*, as a rhythmic and musical unit, only achieves its full value when it is considered within the frame of the poem or the work as a whole. Y. Scalzitti indicates a certain pattern of structure in *Tête d'or* and points to a development in the *verset* from its structurally and syntactically simple form in the first works to the later use of 'la grande aile de l'incidente', particularly in the *versets* of the *Soulier de satin*. This development – 'la phrase en versets brefs fait place au découpage logique de la phrase à grandes ondes: le sens est préféré au sentiment . . .' [64] – from the predominance of the image pattern to that of the thought pattern would bring the *verset* closer to the prosody of the psalms.

When one looks for the influence of Hebrew prosody in Claudel's work, one is more likely to find it in his poetry (lyrical and dramatic) rather than in his translations and adaptations of Biblical texts. As A. Hamman[65] pointed out so aptly: 'Paradoxalement ce n'est pas dans son œuvre exégétique mais dans l'œuvre poétique qu'il est le plus biblique.'

It is generally acknowledged by Old Testament scholars that parallelism in various forms, synonymous, complementary, antithetical, synthetic, is to be regarded as the pattern of Hebrew poetry. It is also agreed that the rhythm of Hebrew poetry is based on a 'sense' or logical unit which coincides with the metrical unit,[66] what Mowinckel[67] calls 'das Gesetz des Gedankenreims'. H. Kosmala[68] submits a number of Biblical texts to close scrutiny, following the principle of the word-thought unit, and shows that the lines are related by a common bond of ideas and follow each other in a certain discernible pattern. As a poet, the psalmist was freer in his manner of composition than the prophet. His lines could be more loosely strung together and – here we have a close analogy with the pattern of Claudel's lyrical passages– could be repeated in the same psalm as a kind of refrain, or they could be reused in other psalms in the same or in a slightly different form. [69] This seems to coincide with what G. Antoine has shown for the *Cinq grandes odes*. The rather loose form of the stanza enables the poet to amplify, repeat, re-echo. It can, however, also misleadingly give the impression of prose; the psalms [70] and the Claudelian *verset* have been regarded as mere prose writing.

We have already referred to the conclusions arrived at by the translators of the Jerusalem Bible with regard to the rhythm of Hebrew poetry. Reviewing the problems involved in translating the psalms into French, R. Schwab stresses the rhythmic inadequacy of earlier translations, rendered into metric verse. This rhythm, based on stress, in a binary or ternary pattern, can be found elsewhere in oriental languages. 'De toute antiquité, l'esprit humain établissait un rapport . . . entre le rythme calqué sur le souffle humain et un ordre juste du monde . . .' [71] The structure of the psalms depends on combinations of '. . . mots-clés et de thèmes-pivots . . . disposés de place en place, aussi bien dans chaque strophe que d'une strophe à l'autre, de psaume en psaume, la répétition et l'alternance deviennent de grands moyens d'action . . .' [72] As a musician, Gélineau came to similar conclusions; he transposed this rhythm – 'Compte variable des syllabes, compte fixe des accents ' [73] – into his settings of the psalms.

Any attempt to deduce the *verset* solely from Hebrew prosody would be shortsighted and misguided. It is perhaps possible to substantiate Claudel's claim to his indebtedness to the prosody of the psalms by some examples.

The *Cantique de Mesa*[74] is conceived by Claudel as a form of inner dialogue, between Mesa and God, following a similar one in the *Book of Job*. The two themes of the first part of the *Cantique* are indicated by what is variably called 'headline anacrusis', 'patron dynamique' or 'répétition anaphorique' [75]. The themes are *Pourquoi* (what is the reason for what happened to Mesa) and *Vous seul* (God alone is responsible for Mesa's life). The two themes are developed in parallel form.

Pourquoi?
    a

Je demande pourquoi cette femme? Pourquoi cette femme
         a   *b*   *a*   *b*

tout à coup avec art sur le bateau, précisément à ce moment qu'il fallait?

We have here an example of incomplete internal parallelism with compensation. [76] Some of the new elements will be found later in the *Cantique* ('sur le bateau' and '. . . moment qu'il fallait' in a modified form). In the development of the second theme, *Vous seul*, a clear synonymous or anaphoric parallelism is used

> Vous seul!
> *a*
>
> Vous n'avez pas demandé mon avis!
> *b*
>
> D'autorité!
> Vous seul en moi tout d'un coup et toutes les portes fermées,
> *a*
>
> Vous avez pris le commandement, que pouvais-je faire?
> *b*
>
> J'ai essayé!

which affects two alternate lines while the initial *vous* remains identical. The break comes in the second line of the *verset* and introduces a new series of parallelisms; the first two follow immediately and the subsequent ones later in the *Cantique:*

> . . . C'est malin avec moi d'être le plus fort!
> Et c'est malin aussi tout d'un coup de m'avoir apporté cette femme, on peut dire que vous l'avez choisie!

The second part of the second line (tout d'un coup cette femme) repeats the second line of the first *verset*. The anaphoric parallelism of 'C'est malin' will be repeated in two *versets* at the end of the first part; this repetition at intervals corresponds to a similar one in the *Book of Job*, from which Claudel quoted two verses[77] at the beginning of the *Cantique*.

The two *versets*

> Quarante jours sur ce bateau et de m'avoir installé en face d'elle
> *a*   *b*   *c*   *d*

Quarante jours en face d'elle sur ce bateau pour que j'aie
   a   *d*   *b*
bien le temps de la regarder, tout à mon aise,
   Celle qu'il fallait.

present an intricate pattern of synonymous and chiastic parallelism
which is however incomplete and compensated by the long
second line, and, in emphatic position, the short third.

One could consider this as the end of a stanza and the new
motif 'un seul moment' as beginning the next one. The poet again
uses the device of starting the *motif* in the second half of the line[78]

Est-ce que nous croyions en elle? un seul moment?
                    a   *b*

Je dis un seul moment.
            b

Un seul moment est-ce que nous avons cru en elle et que le
   b   *a*
bonheur est entre ses bras, comme on dit?

This follows a similar pattern of partly synonymous, partly
chiastic parallelism with a compensatory line. Before the next
parallel *versets* there is an isolated line

J'étais le captif en grinçant des dents qui ne peut pas bouger!

which corresponds to another isolated line earlier on

Comme un coq de combat que l'on apporte dans un panier!

also dividing two parallel *versets*. Both lines are striking in expression and significance for the passage. This type of dividing line or
axis is also found in Biblical prosody.[79] The two *versets* that follow
represent an almost complete summary of all the themes of this
part of the *Cantique*

C'est malin, tout seul, cette femme, de m'avoir planté
quarante jours tout seul en face de cette femme sur le bateau!
Celle qu'il fallait!
C'est malin tout à coup de vous être mis à faire le supérieur
avec moi.

The complete synonymous external parallelism (the only two different words: 'planté = installé', 'le supérieur = d'autorité' are close in meaning, and such changes occur in the psalms) is strengthened by a double internal parallelism: 'tout seul', 'cette femme'. The somewhat loose syntactical structure, alien to French, but natural to Hebrew, is also used elsewhere for rhythmical effects.[80]

The *Cantique de la Vigne*[81] offers examples of anaphoric parallelism frequently found in the psalms.[82] In the first section of the *Cantique*, the poet introduces the theme, centred around the vine, first as a plant and then in its Biblical and liturgical significance. But the first four lines also set a perfectly symmetrical pattern of prosody re-echoed throughout the whole poem

> Ah, si cet homme ne veut pas en cueillir la grappe,
>
> Ah, s'il ne veut pas en respirer les fumées et accoler ardemment ce flanc même de la terre des aïeux qui lui ouvre sa veine libérale,
>
> Ah, s'il veut continuer à faire le juge,
>
> Ah, s'il tient à conserver son petit jugement et sa raison et ne pas se livrer au feu qui de tous côtés en lui craque et part en flammes et en étincelles,

of two parallel *versets*, one short and one long. The beginning of the second *verset* repeats the idea of the first, in somewhat different words and is then amplified.[83] The same anaphoric parallelism occurs again at the beginning of what one might call a new stanza: it follows at the end of the first long sentence spread over seven *versets*.

> Ah, s'il méprise la grappe, il ne fallait pas planter la vigne

This section or stanza contains its own form of external parallelism

> Qui donc a inventé de mettre le feu dans notre verre comme si c'était de l'eau qui tient toute ensemble,
>
> . . .
>
> Qui donc a inventé de mettre le feu dans notre verre, le

feu même et ce jaune-et-rouge qu'on remue dans le four avec un crochet de fer

and ends on a *verset* which unites the two elements of fire and water. The next section or stanza begins again with the same pattern

Ah, s'il ne veut point qu'elle le croie,
          a
Il ne fallait pas . . .
        b
Ah, s'il ne veut pas l'emmener, il ne fallait pas lui prendre
          a   b
la main !
Ah, s'il ne veut pas épuiser la coupe, il ne faut pas y mettre
          a   b
les levres !

introduces a theme of personal human relationship which is then related to the main theme. In the last part of the *Cantique*, Claudel returns to the pattern of the beginning, using the anaphoric parallelism in progressive form

Ah, s'il est avare et s'il n'aime que ces choses . . .
Ah, s'il est lent et patient et circonspect, et si . . . et s'il n'a pas ce grand vide en lui . . .
Ah, s'il a toujours quelque chose à faire. . . .
Ah, qu'il ne mette point les lèvres à cette coupe . . .

The last echo of this line can be found at the very end of the poem and represents a conclusion to the theme introduced in the first line

Ah, s'il tient à rester intact, il ne faut point éteindre le feu !

In concentrating on the structural prosody of the *verset* we have neglected its rhythmic and musical aspect of which Claudel was so keenly aware. 'Nous ne comprendrons rien à la poétique des Psaumes . . . si comme un rythme incessant à l'arrière de notre conscience, nous perdons le sentiment de cette danse sacrée et de ce dialogue avec le son . . .'[84]

If we have attempted to show to what extent Claudel's prosody seems to lean on that of the poetic parts of the Bible we must of course remember that in this, as with regard to other models, the poet has, to use his own terms, translated what he found before him, into his own idiom, the 'Claudélien'.[85]

NOTES

1. 'Mon pays', lecture given in November 1937 and reprinted in *Contacts et circonstances*, Paris: Gallimard, 1947.

2. 'Le Pays de *l'Annonce faite à Marie*' in *France Illustration*, March 1948.

3. *Mémoires improvisés*, Paris: Gallimard, 1954, p. 13.

4. Letter to J. Samson, June 1944, quoted in *Claudel ou le Poète Musicien*, Paris: Milieu du Monde, 1947.

5. Letter to Suarès of December 1908. Claudel used the *Breviarium Monasticum* in the Solesmes edition; cf. M.-F. Guyard, 'La Bible et la Liturgie' in *RHLF.*, 61e/1, 1961.

6. For the Biblical sources of the *Cinq grandes odes* see M.-F. Guyard, *Recherches Claudéliennes*, Paris: Klinksieck, 1963.

7. Letter to J. Rivière, 11.1.1908 in *Jacques Rivière et Paul Claudel. Correspondance 1907–1914*, Paris: Plon, 1926.

8. Letter to J. Rivière, 28.1.1908, ibid.

9. ibid.

10. ibid.

11. Letter to P. de Tonquédec, 13.6.1917, quoted in *Œuvres Complètes, XVIII*, Paris: Gallimard, 1961, p. 270.

12. 'Saint Jérôme' in *Visages Radieux*, Egloff, 1947.

13. 'Nouveaux psaumes français' in *La Table Ronde*, Avril 1955.

14. *Paul Claudel répond les psaumes*, Neuchâtel: Ides et Calendes, 1948.

15. Quoted by P. Rywalski, *La Bible dans l'oeuvre littéraire de Claudel*, Porrentruy: Editions des Portes de France, 1948, p. 21.

16. *J'aime la Bible*, Paris: Fayard, 1955, p. 55.

17. ibid., p. 23.

18. *Ma Conversion* in *Œuvres en Prose*, Pl., Paris, 1965, pp. 1008–14.

19. *Notes sur Mallarmé* (1913), ibid., pp. 513–14.

20. *La Catastrophe d'Igitur* (1926), ibid., pp. 508–13.

21. *Réflexions et Propositions sur le vers français*, ibid., p. 10.

22. ibid., p. 30.

23. ibid.

24. *Journal*, October 1921. Quoted in *Œuvres en Prose*, Pl., (notes), p. 1408.

25. *Réflexions et Propositions sur le vers français*, Pl., p. 38.

26. *Boileau*, (1911), in *Œuvres en Prose*, Pl., pp. 437–8.

27. 'Conversations sur Jean Racine' in *Cahiers Madeleine Renaud-Jean-Louis Barrault*, Paris: Julliard, 1955.

28. ibid.

29. *Mémoires improvisés*, p. 44.

30. One recalls protests against classical prosody from earlier critics: Rapin wrote: 'C'est une beauté inconnue de notre langue dont toutes les syllabes sont comptées dans le vers, car elle n'a nulle diversité de cadence ... la monotonie de notre vers Alexandrin ... me paroist un grand faible dans la Poësie Françoise ...' (*Réflexions sur la poétique*, 1675); Fénelon in his *Lettre à l'académie* noted: 'Notre versification perd plus ... qu'elle ne gagne par les rimes: elle perd beaucoup de variété, de facilité et d'harmonie ...'

31. *Réflexions et propositions sur le vers français*, Pl., pp. 13–14.

32. ibid.

33. Letter to G. Brandes, 1903, quoted in *Œuvres en Prose*, Pl., (notes), pp. 1407–8.

34. Letter to Mockel, December 1890, quoted in *Cahiers Paul Claudel, I*, Paris: Gallimard, 1959, p. 141.

35. *Connaissance du temps*, Pl., p. 141.

36. *Connaissance du temps;* see also M. de Gandillac, ' "Scission" et "connaissance" de Claudel' in *Revue de Métaphysique et de Morale*, 71/4, (1966), 412–25.

37. *Réflexions et propositions sur le vers français*, Pl., p. 3.

38. 'Le Coeur compte' in *Études Carmélitaines*, Sept. 1950.

39. It is perhaps preferable to retain the French terms, since Claudel, rightly or wrongly, attached etymological importance to them.

40. 'Le Coeur compte', loc. cit.

41. Introduction to *l'Orestie d'Eschyle* (1942), Paris: Gallimard, 1961.

42. *Les Psaumes*, trans. R. Tournay and R. Schwab, Paris: Cerf, 1955, Introduction, p. 39.

43. *Réflexions et propositions sur le vers français*, Pl., pp. 37–8.

44. ibid.

45. ibid., p. 3.

46. ibid., p. 38.

47. ibid., pp. 43–4.

48. *Mémoires improvisés*, p. 43.

49. One might recall here that Fénelon stressed the superiority of La Fontaine's *vers irréguliers*, for 'leur inégalité, sans règle uniforme, donne la liberté de

varier leur mesure, et leur cadence, suivant qu'on veut s'élever ou se rabaisser' (*Lettre à l'académie*).

50. *Réflexions et propositions sur le vers français*, Pl., pp. 5–6.
51. *La littérature française contemporaine étudiée dans les textes*, Paris: Colin, 1939, p. 49.
52. J. Madaule, *Le Génie de Paul Claudel*, Paris: Desclee, 1933, pp. 267 ff.
53. C. Chomez, *Introduction à Paul Claudel*, Paris: Albin Michel, 1947, p. 22.
54. J. Samson, *Paul Claudel Poète-Musicien*, Paris: Milieu du Monde, 1947, pp. 91–2.
55. ibid.
56. P. Rywalski, *La Bible dans l'oeuvre littéraire de Paul Claudel*, Porrentruy, 1948. The same point is repeated by A. Czaschke, 'Der "Cantique de Mesa" in Paul Claudel's *Partage de midi*' in *Forschungen zur Romanischen Philologie*, Heft 13, Münster, 1964.
57. Y. Le Hir, 'L'inspiration biblique dans l'*Histoire de Tobie et de Sara*', in *NRF* (Sept. 1955), pp. 440 ff.
58. G. Antoine, 'Les *Cinq grandes odes* ou *la poésie de la répétition*', *Lettres Modernes*, Paris: Minard, 1959.
59. 'Arthur Honegger' in *L'Oeil écoute* (1946), in *Œuvres en prose*, Pl., p. 377
60. 'D'un geste linguistique familier à Claudel' in 'Le Regard en arrière,' *Revue des Lettres Modernes*, II, (1965), pp. 114–16.
61. A. Vachon, *Le Temps et l'Espace dans l'Oeuvre de Paul Claudel*, Paris: Editions du Seuil, 1965, p. 311.
62. ibid.
63. 'Le verset claudelien, une étude du rythme (Tête d'Or)', *Archives des lettres modernes*, 63, (1965–6), pp. 39–40.
64. ibid., p. 69.
65. A. Hamman, 'Un vieil homme qui dévore de l'hébreu' in *La Table Ronde* (Avril 1955), pp. 99–103.
66. W. O. E. Oesterly, *The Psalms*, London: S.P.C.K., 1953, pp. 20–33.
67. S. Mowinckel, 'Marginalien zur hebräischen Metrik', in *ZATW*, 68, (1956), pp. 97–123.
68. 'Ancient Hebrew Poetry', in *Vetus Testamentum*, 14, (1964), pp. 423–45, and 'Form and Structure in Ancient Hebrew', *Vetus Testamentum*, 16, (1966/2), pp. 152–80.
69. 'Form and structure in Ancient Hebrew', loc. cit., p. 176.
70. ibid., p. 178.
71. R. Schwab, 'Nouveaux Psaumes Français' in *La Table Ronde*, (Avril 1955), pp. 146–7.
72. ibid.
73. ibid., p. 146.

74. *Partage de midi*, (version pour la scène), Act III, *Œuvres Complètes, XII*, Paris: Gallimard, 1958.

75. H. Kosmala, art. cit., *Vetus Testamentum* (1966), p. 178 ,W. O. E. Oesterly, op. cit., p. 31, Claudel, *Positions, I*, pp. 30-1, Antoine, 'Les Cinq grandes odes', loc. cit., p. 38.

76. cf. W. O. E. Oesterly, op. cit., p. 22.

77. Job, 38: 16-18: Numquid ingressus es . . .
                  Numquid ingressus es . . .
                  Numquid considerasti . . .
        22: Numquid ingressus es . . .
    31-2: Numquid coniungere . . .
                  Numquid producis . . .

78. See Ps. 77 : 8: Nec fiant, sicut patres eorum, generatio
                    prava et exasperans;
                Generatio quae non direxit cor suum . . .

79. See H. Kosmala, art cit., *Vetus Testamentum* (1964), p. 443, who quotes a similar example from the structure of *Isaiah*, VII, 7-9.

80. ibid.

81. In *La Cantate à trois voix*.

82. Ps. 112:9-10:

Domus Israel speravit in Domino;
adiutor eorum et protector eorum est.
Domus Aaron speravit in Domino;
adiutor eorum et protector eorum est.

A variation of this pattern can be found in Ps. 73:13-17, and one which Claudel frequently uses himself:

Tu confirmasti in virtute tua mare . . .
Tu confregisti capita draconis . . .
Tu dirupisti fontes et torrentes . . .
Tuus est dies, et tua est nox . . .
Tu fecisti omnes terminos terrae . . .

83. See Kosmala, *Vetus Testamentum*, (1966), p. 176.

84. *Les Aventures de Sophie*, Paris: Gallimard, 1937, p. 142.

85. A. du Sarment, *Lettres inédites de mon parrain Paul Claudel*, Paris: Gabalda, 1959, p. 182; the author relates that the poet 'vient de traduire les psaumes en claudélien'.

9 · Claudel and Balzac

GILBERT GADOFFRE

FOR A LONG TIME Claudel did not mention Balzac among the authors who had influenced him in his youth. The journalists who interviewed the author of *L'Otage* and *L'Annonce faite à Marie*, then already a famous ambassador, and asked him which authors had been his masters, received the reply: Aeschylus, Dante, Shakespeare, Dostoyevsky, Rimbaud, and occasionally Bossuet, the only representative of classical French literature who escapes his censure. Balzac is passed over in silence or just mentioned among the representatives of a descriptive literature which, 'from Balzac to Marcel Proust' held the central position in the literary life of that detested nineteenth century.

As he grew older, Claudel modified his views. The cultural francophobia, which had marked his young Symbolist days, abated and gave way to a more moderate assessment of the French past. Who could have foreseen that before his death, the author of *Tête d'or* would pay homage to Racine! In his long dialogue with Amrouche, published under the title of *Mémoires improvisés*, Claudel finally admits that Balzac had meant as much to him in his youth, 'ce qu'était Homère pour les anciens Grecs'. He even goes so far as to acknowledge that he had been 'plus ou moins inconsciemment influencé' by the plot of *Une Ténébreuse Affaire* at the time he was writing l'*Otage*. Without naming Balzac as one of his major literary inspirations, he fully acknowledges his debt to him.

This relationship is less surprising than it at first appears: the two writers are destined to mutual understanding. One is fully aware of everything which separates Tête d'Or, Turelure or Rodrigue from Rastignac and Vautrin, but all of them are conquerors as well as figure-heads of a gigantic and ambitious work. One knows all that Balzac put into these outsize characters, and in Tête d'Or, Avare, Turelure or Rodrigue, one finds the prototype of the Claudelian adventurer, determined from the start to attack the world. For both Claudel and Balzac began life with an obsessional fear of being in the defeated camp. The defeated for Claudel meant such men as Verlaine and Villiers in whom, at the end of their sad lives, he had perceived 'la figure hagarde', and this sight had remained graven in his mind in 'traits ineffaçables'.[1] Claudel always remained a man of the soil at heart, and nothing could shock him more than their 'incompatibilité entre la vision et la réalité, entre le désir et la possibilité'. The vocation of 'poète maudit' was fundamentally 'étrangère à son tempérament'.[2]

The vocation of conqueror, however, implies a realistic evaluation of possibilities, plans for the future, moral sanctions, and solid foundations. Having entered the diplomatic service by way of a competitive examination, at a time when, as the son of a minor treasury official without private means, reputation, connections or impressive personality, he had not the slightest chance of making a successful career there, he immediately chose the realistic solution: specialization in economic affairs where he would find very little competition among the brilliant young men who came from the salons of Paris. It was in this carefully chosen field that he first went into action, and became, in China, the expert who was always sent everywhere where problems of firms or railway construction had to be dealt with, or loans negotiated. This is where he had his first successes. 'S'il n'était diplomate j'en ferais un directeur de chemins de fer', said Émile Francqui, the Belgian business man who had seen him at work.

In the role of poet as well as that of consul, he was a conqueror. He had nothing of the Romantic's loving, filial or passionate submission in the presence of nature. 'La Nature n'est pas notre mère mais notre sœur', Claudel constantly repeated, but a sister who must obey because man is an epitome of the world, the Creator's delegate to the world of knowledge, 'il porte en lui les racines de toutes les forces qui mettent le monde en œuvre, et en constitue l'exemplaire abrégé et le document didactique . . . Avant d'ouvrir les yeux, je sais tout par cœur'.[3] Thus speaks the author of L'Art poétique, and it is not surprising to hear him cry out in the forest of Nikko: 'Je suis l'Inspecteur de la Création, le Vérificateur de la chose présente.'[4] Half-way between God and Earth, the Claudelian hero is a loyal Prometheus who has not had to steal the fire which has been granted him by grace, and does not feel in the least that he is there to submit to Nature, but to conquer it. In this respect he is a man of the twentieth century; indeed very much more so, in spite of his taste for archaic trappings, than some of his seemingly more modern contemporaries. He is not scandalized by the technological age. At the age of sixty, undaunted by visions of the life of the future, he sings, in the *Conversations dans le Loir-et-Cher*, a hymn to the cities of sky-scrapers and of high connecting bridges of which he dreamt as a thing of the future.

But one finds in this new man, who was a product of the social classes which do not look back nostalgically to the past, and who was brought up in an agnostic and aggressively republican environment, as one does in Balzac, an ambivalent attitude towards the French past, which lends itself to contradictory interpretations. People have tried to see in Balzac, sometimes a hardened legitimist regretting the bygone society, sometimes a partisan of the Louis-Philippe *bourgeoisie*, not to say a Marxist. In fact he is all these things at the same time. A new man, his fate is also tied to this rising *bourgeoisie* whose force and dynamism he praises, but at the same time he loves the old order in as much as he can be sure that it will never return; and in so far that it has that unique charm of transitory things which believe themselves to be eternal.

One finds the same ambivalence in Claudel, and more than one critic has fallen into the trap of seeing in *L'Otage* a spokesman for feudal France and the Coufontaine scale of values. One only has to have known Claudel, read his correspondence or his *Mémoires improvisés* to be persuaded of just the contrary. Claudel never made a secret of the fact that he identifies himself, at least partly, with Turelure, and this admission itself reveals certain characteristics which one often fails to stress: a sense of humour - which may turn into black humour when it is called for - and an amazing ability to observe himself with detachment. But having written the last line of *L'Otage*, Claudel became aware of the problem and confided in Gide his fear of seeing his play wrongly interpreted:

> Je suis bien embarrassé par la publication. La plupart des lecteurs superficiels et pressés le prendront pour un livre réactionnaire au sens le plus actuel et le plus contemporain. En réalité, j'ai voulu y donner un spectacle de forces contrariées dont aucune, pas même le Pape qui joue le rôle principal, pas même Dieu, n'a le champ complètement à elle.[5]

Things did in fact turn out as the author had feared, but one must say in defence of the hasty critics, that the fact that Claudel identifies himself with Turelure, in no way excludes ambivalance. To the extent that the Claudelian trilogy, as *La Comédie humaine*, claims to be an epic, it magnifies the defeated and the victims, who rouse the emotions. Who would not take the side of the suffering Sygne? However, Turelure has just said to her that she may well die through pride, in a state almost amounting to impenitence. But terror and pity played in her favour; in a *Ténébreuse Affaire* they similarly played in favour of Laurence de Saint-Sygne, defeated and revolted against God. In both cases, the author offers us a mixture of a nostalgic love for the symbolic forms of the past – the patriarchal monarchy, the Benedictine monastery, the castle, feudal lands – and a secret joy in face of the irrevocable triumph of the forces of life and of history.

Claudel rarely mentions the novel in his prose works, but the little he wrote about Balzac reveals a penetrating insight into the person whom he calls the 'grand entrepreneur de points de vue'. However, he has very little taste for the novel form and the nineteenth century was his nightmare. Surely the prose of Balzac's times aimed at describing, at transcribing rather than explaining? For a whole century, wrote Claudel in *La Catastrophe d'Igitur*, 'depuis Balzac, la littérature avait vécu d'inventaires et de descriptions', and it needed Mallarmé to restore meaning. But Balzac, who works on the material world, is at the same time capable of detaching himself from it. He is one of those, says Claudel, for whom 'l'esprit humain a autorité sur la matière', and who know that 'cette terre est appropriée non seulement à l'exercice de notre sensibilité animale, mais à l'ordre que notre intelligence a pour mission de retrouver'.[6] Above all else, he is a man of the earth; in an attempt to place the great writers under the signs of the elements, Claudel attributes water to Lamartine, fire to Tacitus, the wind to Hugo and earth to Bossuet and Balzac. Just as Bossuet 'du haut de sa chaire ne se lasse pas d'envisager les ondulations majestueuses du grand dessein providentiel' by giving some meaning to the formless chaos of history, Balzac, 'grand entrepreneur de points de vue', is able to bring perspective to the matter which presents itself to him.

> La réalité vraie, celle qui adhère à nos sens et à notre esprit, est tout autre chose que l'enregistrement des événements généraux qui intéressent la nation, la description des institutions, l'analyse des causes et des circonstances qui les suscitent et les modifient, le récit avec accompagnement d'une musique latente ou sourde des évolutions sur la scène publique d'un certain nombre de figures officielles. Il y a d'abord l'ambiance, un certain équilibre, une certaine sensibilité commune à l'état des choses qu'un détail en apparence trivial suffit à caractériser. Il y a surtout le vaste et confus enchevêtrement des drames anonymes et des intérêts particuliers qui se nouent et qui se dénouent au cours de notre propre carrière, la réaction de cette foule à demi-consciente et à demi-aveugle à ce mouvement sous ses pieds qui a un sens. Toutes sortes de comédies se jouent autour de nous, toutes sortes de moralités à demi-formulées, défigurées par des lacunes odieuses et des embarras latéraux, amputées de leurs prémisses et de leurs conclusions se proposent à notre sagacité. L'art du romancier est de retrouver le fil conducteur et de faire un tout, une histoire suivie, de ces linéaments entremêlés. Dans ce travail il est sourdement guidé par ses propres sentiments auxquels le long événement, qu'il a épousé dans la complexe répartition de ses péripéties et de ses personnages, n'est là que pour fournir expression.

Claudel is far from forgetting that this 'fil conducteur' is brought to the surface by the sensibility of the artist: it is up to him to provide the pattern which gives a structure to reality:

> On s'aperçoit bientôt que le conteur, ou pour lui donner son véritable nom le poète, porte avec lui une sorte de patron essentiel, de situation fondamentale, à laquelle tout ce qu'il a pu saisir de la réalité ambiante n'est là que pour fournir illustration, pour remplir de couleurs un cadre préétabli. Il me serait plus facile qu'on ne pourrait croire de démontrer la vérité de cette proposition par l'exemple de Balzac lui-même.[7]

One can see that in this analysis – one of the most penetrating which has ever been written on the creative art of Balzac – the author of *La Comédie humaine* is scarcely distinguished from a poet. His role is to render intelligible, he is 'l'homme qui parle à la place de ce qui se tait autour de lui'[8]; among all the people and situations which he observes, he is able to put his finger on the one with a universal significance, or on 'ces candidats à l'existence que la plume de Balzac ou le crayon d'un Daumier a promu jusqu'à la dignité du type'.[9] Balzac is a poet, even in his language, contrary to what the majority of French critics think, who are inclined to portray the author of *La Comédie humaine* as on the one hand a great creative artist and on the other an appalling stylist. Balzac is 'un admirable écrivain', writes Claudel in *Réflexions et propositions sur le vers français*. And as an example he quotes a very beautiful passage from *Lys dans la vallée*:

> Le souffle de son âme se déployait dans les replis des syllabes, comme le son se divise sous les clés d'une flûte. Sa façon de dire les terminaisons en *i* faisait croire à quelque chant d'oiseau; le *c* prononcé par elle était comme une caresse . . . elle étendait ainsi sans le savoir le sens des mots et vous entraînait dans un monde surhumain.

This quotation comes at the end of a paragraph which, at the time, caused a scandal and in which the author of *Connaissance de l'Est* did not hesitate to claim that the poetic potential of the

French language could be developed more easily in the prose of the great prose-writers than in poetry in the accepted sense:

> Tout ce qu'il y a en français d'invention, de force, de passion, d'éloquence, de rêve, de verve, de couleur, de musique spontanée, de sentiment des grands ensembles, tout ce qui répond le mieux, en un mot, à l'idée que depuis Homère on se fait généralement de la poésie, chez nous ne se trouve pas dans la poésie mais dans la prose. Les grands *poètes français*, les grands créateurs ne s'appellent pas Malherbe ou Despréaux ou Voltaire, ni même Racine, André Chénier, Baudelaire ou Mallarmé. Ils s'appellent Rabelais, Pascal, Bossuet, Saint-Simon, Chateaubriand, Honoré de Balzac, Michelet.[10]

The case of Balzac is thus treated on a general plane, namely that of the potentialities of the French language, and the apologia of the great prose writers is here closely linked to a theory about the very nature of poetry.

NOTES

1. Letter from Claudel to Gide, 2.2.1910, *Correspondance 1899-1926*. Paris: Gallimard, 1949, p. 118.
2. Claudel, 'Paul Verlaine', *Œuvres en prose*, Pl., Paris, 1965, p. 504 (from now on this fourth volume of the collected works of Claudel on the Pléiade edition will be abbreviated to Pl. IV); and 'Diplomatie et poésie', Pl. IV, p. 1501.
3. *Art poétique*, Pl. III, p. 47.
4. 'Le Promeneur', *Connaissance de l'Est*, Pl. III, p. 85.
5. Letter from Claudel to Gide, 2.6.1919, *Correspondance 1899-1926*, p. 137.
6. Claudel, 'Discours sur les Lettres françaises', Pl. IV, p. 663.
7. Claudel, 'Sur Victor Hugo', Pl. IV, p. 470.
8. ibid.
9. ibid.
10. Pl. IV, pp. 43-44; This attack on French classical poetry was answered by Paul Souday in an article in *Temps*, 20.12.1928, saying that Claudel, 'n'a pas le son français: on le dirait toujours traduit de l'ongro-finnois ou du tartare-mandchou'.

10 · Poland in the life and works of Claudel

WITOLD LEITGEBER

WE HAVE MANY PROOFS in Claudel's work of his interest in the foreign countries visited during his long diplomatic career. Poland is the only country in which Claudel has also shown a great interest without ever being there. This is intriguing for any student of his work. In world literature there is no other example of such an interest in Poland by a foreign writer. What could have been the reason? It is not easy to give a ready reply. The sources of a poet's inspiration are very often baffling and difficult to discover. We may only guess and put forward some hypotheses.

First of all one can assume that the fact that Poland was such a strongly Catholic country must have attracted his attention and interest. He felt curious about Poland, particularly where the religious aspects of her history are concerned. He interprets this history from the point of view of a believer. However, Claudel was conversant not only with the history of Poland but also with many other of her facets. This interest is shown in many of his observations, some short and scattered throughout his prolific output. These testify to his deep understanding of Poland's role in the world, and especially of her struggle for independence. Of course here and there one may question some of his opinions and disagree with some of the facts set down. Nevertheless, Claudel's warm feeling towards Poland characterized all his writings.[1]

Amongst the many such observations on Poland in Claudel's prose we may mention the book *Contacts et circonstances* where, in his reflections 'Témoignage' Claudel spoke of the partition of Poland as the mortal sin of Europe, and of the terrible punishment meted out by Providence to 'les trois Empires criminels qui y ont participé'.[2] He interpreted this as proof of the immanent justice which exists in the world. In the same volume there is an article which appeared originally in *Le Figaro* of 28 May 1938, on the situation of Austria and Poland at this period of great international tension. In it he wrote:

> Mais me sera-t-il permis de dire que ma pensée va spécialement aujourd'hui à cette nation chrétienne à laquelle me rattachent tant de liens, qui pendant plus d'un siècle a infatigablement confessé le Christ et revendiqué le droit sous les pieds d'un triple envahisseur, je veux dire la Pologne? Tous mes amis de là-bas n'ont pas oublié qu'au plus sombre de cette histoire héroïque, quand la résurrection semblait le plus invraisemblable des miracles, il y a eu un poète français pour proclamer sa foi dans 'le Peuple divisé'.[3]

In his *Au milieu des vitraux de l'Apocalypse*, he again wrote about the martyrdom of Poland, citing her among the examples of God's people in captivity, 'C'est Israël en Egypte, c'est Juda en captivité, c'est la chrétienté Romaine des premiers siècles, c'est la Pologne et l'Irlande martyrisées . . .'[4] Moreover, in his *Mémoires improvisés* he speaks of 'le sacrifice qui a été consommé par Hedwige et Jagellon en Pologne'.[5] This episode of Polish history in the fourteenth century must have made a great impression on Claudel as an example of perfect sacrifice in response to God's calling. This is a subject very dear to the poet's heart and a theme which is the subject of many of his works, particularly the plays. Finally on another occasion he wrote: 'Vienne, clef de l'Europe, n'échappait que de justesse à l'assaut des Turcs, grâce au dévouement de Sobieski'[6] – the episode in Polish history which had caught Claudel's attention, when King Jan Sobieski had saved Christian Europe in 1683.

Shortly after the outbreak of the Second World War Claudel spoke on the French radio to the German people, giving expression to his indignation at the fate of Poland, 'l'indignation d'une conscience revoltée à la vue d'un peuple innocent lâchement assassiné dans les conditions les plus infâmes'.[7] Some time later Claudel wrote in *Le Figaro Littéraire*, giving expression to his doubts about the durability, as he ironically put, of 'la Maison

Hitler' as well as of 'la Maison Staline', further manifesting his grief that France was unable to come to the aid of a Poland, 'qui s'engloutit sous nos yeux dans des conditions atroces'. In conclusion, Claudel stressed that 'nous aurons besoin dans l'avenir de la Pologne à qui nous avons fait des promesses sacrées'.[8]

From the same period there exists his beautiful oration* in which it is apparent that he looks on the defeat of Poland through the eyes of Biblical Prophets, and interprets Poland's disasters in his own characteristic way as an exegete of the Holy Scripture. Poland was a victim, like others of God's peoples before, constantly preyed upon by the Beast of the Apocalypse. God seems to be silent for the moment, to test the victim. But Claudel believes in the resurrection of Poland, because 'il y a Dieu qui est le plus fort', and the walls of Babylon will crumble.

PARTAGE DE MIDI

The other reason – perhaps the main one – for Claudel's interest in Poland which found expression in his poetic and dramatic works was, as one may suppose, a personal experience – namely his meeting with a Polish woman. This meeting first led him away from his chosen path in life, but later pointed the right direction for him to follow.

In 1900 Claudel spent some weeks in the famous Benedictine abbeys at Solesmes and Ligugé. His long inner conflict between the desire to devote his life to God, his artistic vocation and his chosen diplomatic career, had reached a climax, and he decided to enter the monastery. His request was, however, met with the advice to delay such an irrevocable step. Claudel took this as being a definite refusal and it deeply depressed him. He was near breaking point and felt as if his whole world had suddenly fallen apart.

In this depressed frame of mind Claudel left France in October 1900. He boarded the *Ernest Simmons* for China to take up the post of Consul in Foochow. During the voyage some new passengers embarked at Ile de la Réunion – a Polish woman of

* See the text, published for the first time at the end of this article.

great beauty with her husband, a foreigner, and four young children. This is the Ysé of his future play, whose real name was Rose.[9] It is interesting to note that the symbol of the rose often appears throughout Claudel's work, amongst others in *Cinq grandes odes*. During the long voyage Claudel met this woman, and had long discussions with her on the Bible and on *Of the Imitation of Christ* – a subject on which she seemed to be well versed. Claudel's deeply religious interests contrasted strangely with her gay and light-hearted personality. The young Consul and would-be monk, did not, however, remain indifferent to the charms of a beautiful woman. One evening there was a party on board, in which the passengers played the traditional English party-game called 'Hunt the Slipper'. The reward was a dance with the owner of the slipper. Claudel was the lucky winner, and thus began a romance which lasted for four years of Claudel's stay in Foochow. The outcome was a child; but even though she later became a widow, Rose refused to marry Claudel.[10] In August 1904 she left Foochow as she did not want to be an obstacle to his religious vocation. When Claudel returned to France the following year, and tried to contact her in Brussels in April 1905, she evaded him, leaving on her front door a medallion of St Benedict. In this way she no doubt wanted to remind Claudel of that which he was probably trying to forget.[11] But let us not go into any further detail in respect to those who are still alive.[12] In 1906, Claudel married a Frenchwoman who survived him.

Claudel's romance with the beautiful Pole found full poetic expression in *Partage de midi*.[13] The play was written 'with my own blood', as he confessed in the autumn of 1905, shortly after deeply felt experiences. Through this drama one can understand both the great importance of this meeting in Claudel's spiritual life, and its deep influence on his creative work. In the eyes of the poet this meeting was the second intervention of God in his life, following his conversion in 1886, which was of dominant importance.

In *Partage de midi* Claudel analyses the mysterious role which human love plays in relations between men and women and, in particular, he examines the 'impossible love' forbidden by Law. He was also meditating on the problem of why God, who himself is Love, allows such temptation; what is the meaning of it?

He did not find the answer immediately. For that twenty more years were needed. In *Le Soulier de satin* (the title reminds us of the slipper on board ship) Claudel fully understood that 'even sins' – *Etiam peccata*, could play a role in the economy of salvation. Forbidden love, through renunciation and sacrifice, can become a powerful force which moves man to 'tenter l'impossible' and can lead to 'délivrance aux âmes captives' – as can be read in the last words of *Le Soulier de satin*. Ysé re-appeared in *Le Soulier de satin* as Prouhèze – this time, however, she is responsible for the hero's salvation, not his fall.

Even though the action of this play takes place in Spain, Claudel did not forget Poland. He made Prouhèze's important letter to her beloved Rodrigue pass through Poland during its long voyage all over the world.[14] So, too, in *Le Soulier de satin* can some echo be found of Claudel's interest in Poland.

Claudel finished writing *Le Soulier de satin* in Japan where he was the French Ambassador. During the great earthquake of 1 September 1923, the Embassy building in Tokyo was completely destroyed. Claudel miraculously escaped with his family. Many of his manuscripts, however, were destroyed, including the third part of *Le Soulier de satin*, in which Poland is mentioned. Claudel and his family, having lost the roof over their heads and all their belongings, found refuge in the Polish Embassy which by chance had not been destroyed.[15]

To return to *Partage de midi*, Claudel refused permission to stage this play for over forty years, in spite of the insistent demands by producers. Not until 1948 did he consent to a production by Jean-Louis Barrault, who played such a great part in introducing Claudel's dramas to the post-war stage. The performance in Paris was attended not only by Claudel's wife, but also by the real Ysé.[16] With the passage of time long-past events fell into the background, and the artistic work remained. In the same year *Partage de midi*, previously only printed privately in a

special edition exclusively for Claudel's friends, was re-issued for
the first time to the public. There were two versions, one original
and the second for the stage. It is characteristic that in the author's
stage instructions for the third act of the latter, Claudel for the
first time hinted at Ysé's nationality. He instructed that on the
table at which Ysé is sitting on the stage, a reproduction of the
famous Polish Madonna, Our Lady of Czestochowa should stand
between two candles.[17] This detail was not included in the
original version.

LA CANTATE À TROIS VOIX

Love, separation and exile, sacrifice and liberation – these are
the themes which weave constantly through Claudel's works. The
poet, who looks at the world with the eyes of a believer, tries to
solve the riddle of human existence. He meditates on these subjects both in his dramas and his poetical works.

In the years 1911–12, Claudel wrote *La Cantate à trois voix*,
which is also concerned with these problems, and where one of
the voices is a Polish one.

On a June midnight, at 'Cette heure qui est entre le printemps
et l'été',[18] three young women are sitting on the banks of the
Rhône, looking at a magnificent spectacle of nature. These are:
Laeta, representing the Latin race, betrothed and awaiting her
beloved; Fausta, Polish, separated from her husband, and Beata,
Egyptian, widowed soon after her wedding. All three as they look
at the world surrounding them, dream and talk about their fate.
Breaking off their conversation from time to time they give
expression to their feelings and thoughts in 'cantiques'. In these
canticles they sing about those absent. The fact that they are
separated leads them to search for God. All three try to discover
the transitional image of eternal happiness in the glory of 'passing
things' and in the memory of 'temporary happiness'.

In no other work did Claudel express the most mysterious
problems of human existence with such a wealth of imagery and
metaphors, and in words more gripping and penetrating, and at
the same time beautiful, than in *La Cantate à trois voix*.

As regards Fausta, the Polish woman, she is exiled from her native country. She belongs to a 'peuple divisé', about whom she sings in one of her 'cantiques'. This is one of the most beautiful poems about Poland ever written by a non-Polish poet:[19]

> Entre l'Orient et l'Occident, là où les eaux se partagent sans pente,
> Au centre de l'Europe il y a un peuple divisé.
> . . . Au centre de trois peuples il y a un peuple submergé.
> Dieu l'a voulu ainsi afin qu'entre l'Est et l'Ouest, entre l'hérésie et le schisme, là où l'Europe s'arrache en trois morceaux,
> Il y ait un sacrifice perpétuel et un peuple selon son cœur:
> Et le nom même de la Pologne n'est pas retrouvé sur la carte . . .[20]

Fausta was separated from her country and husband by the demands of patriotism. Her husband was away, in faraway Poland, concerned with their country's cause. She herself was living in a foreign land, 'une terre qui n'est pas la mienne'. She was in charge of a national fund serving both the Polish cause and her husband, in order to keep him alive. Fausta speaks bitterly about the pain of desire which can be satisfied neither by the beauty of the world, nor by the fulfilment of human love. If her beloved returned to morrow, should she open her heart and show her love? She will not do this, as he will not open his heart. Both belong to the Polish cause alone.[21] Fausta must forbear affection because this could turn her husband away from his patriotic duties. He, too, is not allowed to show his love, because this could take away Fausta's courage to endure. So – as the poet says – sacrifice is necessary in order to accomplish great deeds. Fausta symbolizes Ceres, a ripe harvest, which will soon be transformed into gold. She symbolizes the whole of mankind aspiring to God.

Before Claudel published the whole of *La Cantate à trois voix*, he first printed part of it, in fact Fausta's song about the 'peuple divisé'. It appeared in 1913 in *la Nouvelle Revue Française* under the title of 'Cantique de la Pologne'.

Lumîr, who is also Polish and one of the main characters of the drama *Le Pain dur*, is partly derived from Fausta.

LE PAIN DUR

Le Pain dur forms the second part of Claudel's dramatic trilogy. The first part, as we know, is *L'Otage*, and the third *Le Père humilié*. This trilogy was written in the years 1909–16, or perhaps 1917. It is a poetic reflection on the nineteenth century: its historical events, upheavals and problems symbolized in the story of the life of three generations of the family of an upstart and renegade, Turelure. Claudel wanted to show in these three dramas the significance of this epoch, the influence of the French revolution on the spiritual, political, social and economic order of that period. At the same time he wanted to stress the continued presence and existence of the Church, in spite of all the cataclysms which may shake the barque of St Peter.

Through these people and events Claudel revealed the reciprocal influence on the world's history of tradition and progress, of old and new, of things lasting and changing. The poet shows equal understanding for that which passes away, and that which is being born. He seems to advocate the acceptance of the future, even though this future may be taking a repugnant form. He seems to say that we must accept that which is creative and adapt it. In this respect Claudel's attitude appears to be very much in the spirit known nowadays as *aggiornamento*.

Claudel's trilogy was called a 'Christian Oresteia' which tells the story of the Turelure family (House of Atreus), full of cruelties. However, as in the Aeschylus trilogy the tragic events lead in the end to purification and the abolition of the inexorable, until now, law of vengeance and the spilling of blood. Thus in Claudel's work the whole series of crimes reaches its conclusion in the establishment of peace, and the breaking down of the barriers between aristocratic idealism and *bourgeois* materialism – and at the same time between Judaism and Christianism. Claudel was not the translator of the Aeschylus trilogy for nothing.[22]

The action of *Le Pain dur* takes place in the reign of Louis Philippe. In it Claudel is mostly concerned with the problem of the breaking down of barriers and of the meeting of races and different nationalities, and also with the problem of faith and unbelief. The period 1830–48 saw the beginnings of large-scale industrialization and capitalism; years of technical inventions and colonial expansion. At the same time it was a world of hatred, heartlessness and, above all, a world without God, who seemed to be absent and silent. People stripped each other of love and money. The crucifix, which during the whole action of the play lies abandoned on the stage, will later be sold, its price being dictated solely by the weight of the metal from which it was made.

Into this vortex of passion the young Polish girl, Lumîr, is hurled.[23] Her vocation is her own country, and she is led by patriotic demands, without considering the price, even if this should mean committing a crime. Lumîr is not of such purity as Fausta, in spite of many similarities, such as exile, separation and trusteeship of a national fund. However, Lumîr seems to take part in the drama almost against her will. She feels the strangeness of her environment. She is isolated and later on seems to awake from the nightmare, departing at the end of the play. Claudel probably wanted to stress in this way, that such an exclusive love of one's country left her no place in this world. She could never be happy here. If we revert to the comparison with the Aeschylus trilogy, Lumîr could be Iphigeneia.

In his preparatory notes to *Le Pain dur*, Claudel characterized Lumîr as follows: 'Polonaise. Elle trompe et fait semblant d'aimer. Sa vocation est la patrie. Contre tout, sans aucun espoir, la mort'.[24] Later on, however, during the writing of the play, this character was subject to some changes. Finally Lumîr represents many things in this drama – on the one hand love, fidelity, liberty and willingness to serve, and on the other she is the embodiment of things past and also of danger and death. She remains above all the symbol of vanquished, but unconquerable, patriotism and Claudel concentrates on her in dealing with the problem of love of one's country and the problem of national persecutions. In Lumîr we can see what role Poland played in Claudel's vision of nineteenth-century Europe – spiritual as well as political.

In Act II there is a characteristic dialogue. Turelure's son, Louis, a colonist from Algeria and Lumîr's companion voices at one point the opinion that the country where one lives is one's fatherland and derisively asks her: 'What after all is this Poland of yours?' Lumîr answers with a declaration of her patriotic love. She paints one image after another, which together form her idea of Poland:

La Pologne, pour moi, c'est cette raie rose dans la neige, là-bas, pendant que nous fuyions,

Chassés de notre pays par un autre plus fort,

Cette raie dans la neige, éternellement!

J'étais toute petite alors, blottie dans les fourrures de mon père.

Et je me souviens aussi de cette réunion, la nuit, alors que la révolte commença.

Mon père me prit dans mon lit et m'apporta au milieu de ces hommes armés, tous gentilshommes,

Et il me leva tout debout comme il aimait à le faire, mes deux pieds dans ses fortes mains,

Toute droite dans ma longue chemise blanche et mes cheveux bruns répandus,

Comme une petite statue de l'Espérance et de la Victoire!

Et tous ces hommes fiers autour de moi, les sabres dégainés, criant hourra![25]

Such pictures may well recall the lithographs by the distinguished Polish artist Artur Grottger (1837–67): 'Lithuania', 'Polonia', 'War'. These lithographs represented scenes of Polish insurgents, and were known in reproduction throughout Europe towards the end of the last century. It is quite possible that Claudel knew them too.

Claudel wrote Le Pain dur on the eve of the First World War during his sojourn in Germany as French Consul-General in

Frankfurt and Hamburg. This stay was not without its influence as far as national problems were concerned and in particular the Jewish question. As regards the Polish question, Claudel's meeting with a Polish woman, Maria Dohrn, née Baranowska, was of importance[26]. She was the wife of a well-known German zoologist, Anton Dohrn, and mother of Wolf Dohrn, one of the founders of the Arts Institute at Hellerau, near Dresden, where in 1913 *L'Annonce fait à Marie* was produced.

Maria Dohrn divided her time between Hellerau and the family estate at Wydranka in Russia, in the province of Mogilev, which had formed part of the Kingdom of Poland before partition. In Germany she had many conversations with Claudel on Poland and the Poles. Later she corresponded with him for many years. Several of her letters in French still exist. They are very beautiful, profound and at the same time they prove that the relations between her and Claudel were very close and sincere. These letters, which were never published, and with which I was able to familiarize myself thanks to the kind permission of the Claudel family, were written from Wydranka between 1914–17. Besides personal affairs their main subject was Poland and the problems of faith, the love of God and love of the fatherland, the complex question of nationalities (Poles, Russians, White-Ruthenians and Jews), the difference of culture, customs and religion (Roman and Uniat Catholicism, Russian-Orthodoxy, Judaism). All these problems she knew from her own experience living in a country where they existed in reality. Moreover, Maria Dohrn describes in her letters the history of her family, three generations of which had settled in Wydranka, until after the defeat of the Polish insurrection against Russia in 1863, when her parents had to flee abroad with the little girl. As it appears from this correspondence, she had discussed these subjects with Claudel in Germany, and later wrote on them at his request, very often in reply to specific questions. One of the letters includes a list of endearments such as 'mój kotku' (mon petit chat), which was used by Claudel in the Polish form in *Le Pain dur*.[27] There was also a whole list of Polish girls' names. Apparently Claudel was trying to find a name for his Polish character. Why Claudel chose the name of 'Lumîr', which sounds so strange to Polish ears and which of course was not on the list, seems inexplicable.[28]

'Lumîr' is a name of a Czech legendary bard. Claudel must have known that because during his earlier stay in Prague (1909–11) as the French consul there he became well acquainted with the history and problems of the Slav world, particularly of Bohemia and Poland.[29] At that time a well-known Czech literary periodical was being published in Prague under the name of *Lumîr*. It printed many translations of French literary works.

Reverting to Claudel's correspondence, it is clear from its contents in which matters he was interested, and what influence Maria Baranowska-Dohrn's letters might have had on the composition of *Le Pain dur*.

LE PÈRE HUMILIÉ

In the last part of the trilogy, *Le Père humilié*, there is another short mention of Lumîr. We learn that her surname was Posadowsky, and that she died in Poland in unspecified but sad circumstances – 'elle est mort tristement'.[30] It can only be supposed that she died from persecution by the Russians. Moreover, there is another Polish character in this play, 'Prince Wronsky'[31] who is linked in some way with Lumîr because he wears a cameo with her likeness. The action of the play begins in 1869 with a farewell ball in the gardens of his villa in Rome, which will be auctioned the following day. It is here, in the Polish aristocrat's gardens that the future action of the play is being established. Prince Wronsky is presented as a noble Polish figure; he has many Polish characteristics. He is a one-time insurgent and now an émigré. A certain resignation and bitter pride emanate from him. He lives in the past, nostalgically recalling his native country and youth spent on his family estate not far from the river Dnieper (Claudel uses the ancient French name Borysthène).[32] He can still hear the roar of its waters in Rome. 'Mon pays était sur terre la Pologne pour laquelle il n'y a plus d'espérance',[33] confesses Wronsky.

Here one can find some further echoes of the correspondence

between Claudel and Maria Dohrn, who often wrote about Poland's tragic fate, and whose estate at Wydranka was also situated near the river Dnieper, as often mentioned in her letters.

The figure of Prince Wronsky, although of secondary importance in the play, is another example of Claudel's interest in Poland and the Polish people. He tried to understand them, and had a great deal of warm feeling for them. Claudel never visited Poland, however, although he dearly wanted to go there as I was assured on two occasions by his widow. He would have liked to have been sent to Warsaw as a member of the French diplomatic mission there.

From reminiscences on Claudel in the twenties, published in a Polish periodical, we learn that when once asked why he was not being sent to Warsaw, as he wished, he replied sadly: 'They say that I would do there what the Poles want and that I would be a Polish Ambassador in France rather than a French Minister in Poland', and then he added with a smile: 'And you know, perhaps there is something in that.'[34]

And so Poland existed for ever only in his thoughts and his works.

In Poland, Claudel's works were first translated as early as 1913 when *L'Annonce faite à Marie* appeared in print, to be followed in 1918 by *Cette heure qui est entre le printemps et l'été*, and later on by some other dramas or works of poetry.

The first stage performance took place in newly independent Poland in 1924. A theatre in Cracow presented *l'Annonce faite à Marie*, in a new translation. Then two Warsaw theatres presented *L'Échange* and *Le Repos du septième jour*. The latter play was performed in 1928, thirty-eight years before the Paris première.

During the last war all theatres in Poland under the German occupation were closed. We know, however, of some clandestine meetings in Warsaw and elsewhere at which Claudel's works were read to the great enthusiasm of those present.

At that time some new translations had been made in occupied Poland, among others of *Tête d'or* and *La Ville*, but the manuscripts were unfortunately lost during the Warsaw rising. Only a new translation of *L'Annonce faite à Marie* survived in part. It was completed later and this text served for performances given after the war in London by a Polish student theatre.

In Poland after the last war only *Jeanne d'Arc au bûcher* was given in concert form in Poznan. There were also some performances of *L'Annonce* and *La Jeune Fille Violaine* given by Catholic theatre groups.

In this centenary year, Teatr Polski in Warsaw is planning to stage for the first time *Partage de midi*, in a recent translation.[35]

Of Claudel's many religious works, only *J'aime la Bible* has been translated into Polish, and published in 1958. Save for this one book, there is no Polish edition of Claudel's works available at present. The first translations of his dramas have been out of print for very many years now, and the translations of some of his poems are scattered through various periodicals.

NOTES

1. Claudel in an interview in 1925 with Jaroslaw Iwaszkiewicz, one of his Polish translators, said: 'For a long time Poland for me has been something very alive. I have always been deeply interested in her and took her to my heart. How much strength Poland has shown during those long years, how much faith. But how much strength she still needs in her present position, in her geographical situation. How much faith in herself and in the value of her great destiny. The deep devotion to God's cause and the cause of peace – these are the two characteristics of Poland which inspire my confidence in her future. But you too must have trust and faith. . . .' (Published in a Polish literary weekly, *Wiadomosci Literackie*, Warsaw, 1925, No. 86.)

2. *Œuvres en prose*, Pl., Paris, 1965, p. 1389.

3. 'L'Enfant Jésus de Prague' in *Contacts et circonstances*, Paris: Gallimard, 1947, p. 206. This text was not included in *Œuvres en prose*.

4. *Au milieu des vitraux de l'Apocalypse*, Paris: Gallimard, 1966, p. 196. See also Claudel's letter to André Gide from Tiensin, 30.7.1908, in which he wrote about 'The horrors committed in Poland by the Orthodox clergy', (*The Correspondence, 1899–1926, between Paul Claudel and André Gide*, trans. by John Russell, London: Secker & Warburg, 1952, pp. 74, 250). However, the particular case of 'nuns of Minsk' mentioned by Claudel was later

proved false by the Polish Jesuit, Father J. Urban (*Makryna Mieczyslawska w świetle prawdy*, Cracow: 1923).

5. *Mémoires improvisés*, Paris: Gallimard, 1954, p. 250.
6. 'Claudel diplomate', *Cahier Paul Claudel, No. 4*, Paris: Gallimard, 1962, p. 297.
7. ibid., p. 276.
8. ibid., pp. 284, 288, 289.
9. *Bulletin de la Société Paul Claudel, No. 26*, p. 25.
10. Louis Chaigne, *Vie de Paul Claudel et genèse de son oeuvre*, Tours: Mame, 1961, p. 85. See also '*Le Rire de Paul Claudel*', *Cahier Paul Claudel, No. 2*, Paris: Gallimard, 1960, p. 211, and *Cahiers Paul Claudel, No. 4*, op. cit., p. 111. Paul-André Lesort, *Paul Claudel par lui-meme*, Paris: Ed. du Seuil, 1963, pp. 48, 150. Stanislas Fumet, *Claudel*, Paris: Gallimard, 1958, pp. 68, 72.
11. François Varillon, 'Une Lettre inédite de Paul Claudel', *Études*, (Sept. 1966), p. 225.
12. *Mémoires improvisés*, p. 174.
13. ibid., particularly pp. 38, 158, 166, 180, 187, 311. See also Claudel's letter of 1912 to Marie Kalff cit. in *Bulletin de la Société Paul Claudel, No. 24*, p. 27.
14. *Théâtre II*, Paris: Pl., 1956, p. 821.
15. Zbigniew Bienkowski, 'Paul Claudel', *Tworczosc*, Warsaw, April 1955, p. 200. See also, *Oeuvres en prose*, p. 1145.
16. *Bulletin de la Société Paul Claudel, No. 24*, p. 27.
17. *Théâtre I*, Paris: Pl., 1956, p. 1123.
18. *Œuvre poétique*, Paris: Pl., 1957, p. 321.
19. The Primate of Poland, Cardinal A. Hlond wrote to Claudel, 10.5.1943, from Abbaye d'Hautecombe (Savoie), about *Cantate à trois voix*: 'Comme il est de nouveau actuel après 32 ans, comme il est vrai et vivant . . . Ainsi donc encore une fois. La situation va changer bientôt, radicalement et pour toujours. Cependant cette partie inspirée de la *Cantate à trois voix* restera à jamais dans la littérature mondiale et dans le trésor spirituel de la nation martyre comme un bijou de la plus haute valeur' (Archives P. Claudel, Paris).
20. *Œuvre Poétique*, Pl., p. 340.
21. Wiktor Weintraub, professor of Polish literature at Harvard in a study in English 'Two Parallels', included in the book *Adam Mickiewicz. Ksiega w stulecie zgonu* (London: Veritas, 1957), pp. 503–8, sees in *Cantique du peuple divisé* some convergence of basic ideological tenets with the national Polish Messianism as expressed by the great Polish poet Mickiewicz in his *The Books of the Polish Nation and of the Polish Pilgrimage*. He also sees in Claudel's poem some allusions pointing towards Mickiewicz's poem 'Konrad Wallenrod'. It should be added that *The Books* . . . were first pub-

lished in Polish in Paris in 1832 and in the next year in French, translated by Montalembert. *Konrad Wallenrod* was translated into French in 1881. Claudel therefore might have known these works at the time of writing *La Cantate à trois voix*. However, in an interview given to Maria Petry (*Tygodnik Powszechny*, No. 32 Cracow, 1949) Claudel confessed to his ignorance of Polish literature. He said that he had browsed in *Le Livre des Pélerins Polonais* and did not like Mickiewicz's religious ideas. Moreover this was a 1947 edition of *Le Livre* . . . (Paris: Egloff, 1947); text presented by Mgr Charles Journet and therefore published over 30 years after Claudel had written *Cantique du peuple devisé*.

22. W. H. Matheson, *Claudel and Aeschylus* (University of Michigan Press, 1966), reviewed by Pierre Aquilon, *Bulletin de la Société Paul Claudel, No. 25*, pp. 23–4. Pierre Claudel, 'Le Pain dur à Limoges', *Bulletin de la Société Paul Claudel, No. 22*, p. 10.

23. *Théâtre II*, Pl., pp. 415, 417, 424, 429, 439, 443, 446, 461–2, 465, 466–7, 471.

24. J. Petit, 'Notes sur une genèse', II, *Bulletin de la Société Paul Claudel, No. 2*, pp. 11–13, and Jean-Pierre Kempf et Jacques Petit, *Études sur la 'Trilogie' de Claudel. 2. Le Pain dur*, Paris: Minard, 1967, pp. 26–8.

25. *Théâtre II*, p. 443.

26. Claudel wrote to Gide from Hellerau, 22.9.1913: 'I've found some wonderful souls here, a young Jew and an elderly Polish lady. There is something really amazing in the way people need God today' (op. cit.). Jean-Pierre Kempf et Jacques Petit, op. cit., p. 7, and *Bulletin de la Société Paul Claudel, No. 2*, p. 11. In both sources the name Dohrn is misspelt as 'Dhorn'.

27. *Théâtre II*, p. 465.

28. W. Weintraub, op. cit., p. 507, writes: ' "Lumîr" sounds rather strange to Polish ears. The girl's aunt bears the name of "Kokloschkine" which sounds like a Russian name, formed most probably after the popular Russian surname Kokoshkin . . . The name Wronsky in *Le Père humilié* might have been suggested by that of a romantic Polish philosopher writing in French, Hoene-Wronski, as well as by the well-known character in *Anna Karenina*. In any case, the spelling is that of Russian names in French.' The same may be said of Lumîr's surname 'Posadowsky'. In a letter from Anna Zahorska, a Polish translator and author of a study of his works, written to Claudel in 1927, the following passage appears: 'Je ne veux pas vous pardonner seulement cette abominable Lumîr – nos femmes ne sont pas comme ça – vous avez peint là une Russe, pas une Polonaise' (Archives P. Claudel, Paris). In my opinion all these 'Russian influences' were due at least partly to the fact that some of Claudel's Polish friends were from formerly Polish provinces now belonging to Russia and that

through them there might have been some indirect, involuntary, Russian influence.

29. *Paul Claudel*, Paris: Bibliothèque Nationale, 1968, p. 71. The Catalogue of the recent Paris exhibition of documents concerning P. Claudel.
30. *Théâtre II*, p. 494.
31. See note 28.
32. *Théâtre II*, p. 498.
33. ibid., p. 499.
34. Maria Kasterska, 'My souvenirs of Claudel', in a Polish literary weekly, *Wiadomosci*, No. 475, London, 1955.
35. This plan it seems has fallen through as a result of the new anti-liberal trends in the cultural policy of the Warsaw régime after the revolt in Polish intellectual circles. As reported by Bernard Margueritte, Warsaw Correspondent of *Le Monde*, Paris, 28.2.68.

11 · Pour une Réunion Franco-Polonaise

PAUL CLAUDEL

MADAME BONVOISIN m'a prié de vous dire quelques mots qui servent de préface à cette belle réunion où l'art Polonais va vous faire entendre ses accents les plus melodieux et les plus pathétiques. Ces paroles, je les chercherais en vain au fond d'un coeur pétrifié par l'horreur, et pourquoi ne pas le dire? par le scandale. Dieu agrée les gémissements, et disons même le reproche, des justes opprimés, il écoute, et le ciel même fait silence pour écouter, les plaintes de Job et de Jérémie. Et nous, pendant un mois, nous avons vu une nation généreuse et héroïque, la nation qui pendant des siècles, entre l'hérésie et le schisme, a été le représentant et le champion de la civilisation catholique, enfoncée, défoncée, écrasée, déchirée, humiliée par le poids irrésistible des masses bestiales. Nous avons assisté une fois de plus à ce spectacle consternant de l'esprit vaincu et terrassé par la matière. Nous avons vu brûler le sanctuaire de la Vierge Noire, nous avons assisté, l'oreille tendue à la radio, au massacre de Varsovie. L'aviation ennemie a pu sans obstacle déverser sur des villes et des villages sans défense, sur un peuple abandonné et trahi, ces torrents de fer et de feu qui ont été prédits par les prophètes. Les Panzer-divisionen ont pu sur un sol durci par un été exceptionnel pénétrer jusqu'au coeur du pays et prendre à revers des troupes héroïques mais mal préparées. Et maintenant le silence s'est fait, la barbarie et le crime ont fait alliance une fois de plus, la Bête règne de la Baltique aux Carpathes, tout un peuple de 30 millions d'âmes a été réduit en esclavage, comme aux temps de l'Assyrie, et de ces multitudes qui se tordent sous le fouet de l'exacteur, s'élève non plus même un cri, mais un gémissement: Quare obdormis Domine? Seigneur, qu'est-ce donc qui Vous est arrivé? Faut-il croire que Vous dormez? Est-ce que ces abominations sous Vos yeux ne suffisent pas? N'est-ce pas Vous que l'on appelle le Vengeur et le juste Juge? Et si ce défi monstrueux à

toute idée de moralité et de justice, si le spectacle qu'offre actuelle-
ment la Pologne ne suffit pas, alors qu'est-ce qu'il faudra pour
Vous réveiller?

Mais le Seigneur a déjà repondu. Ce n'est pas première fois
que Gog et Magog ont fait leur apparition dans l'histoire. Le
vieil Ézéchiel parle avant que S. Jean ne reprenne ces noms
maudits pour les suspendre au dessus des dernières pages de son
Apocalypse. Gog, au dire de tous les commentateurs, c'est ce
pays qui était autrefois la Scythie et qui est aujourd'hui la Russie,
et il est remarquable que les plus anciennes versions de la Bible
lui attribuent le nom de Ross ou Russ. C'est le représentant de la
barbarie, et parmi les peuples que ses hordes débordées entraînent
avec elles on relève le nom de Thogorma, que le jésuite Meno-
chius, qui florissait au XVIe siècle n'hésite pas à traduire par
Germani, les Allemands! 'Les Rois de la Terre, disait déjà le
Psalmiste, se sont levés et les chefs se sont entendus contre le
Seigneur et contre son Christ.' La haine de Dieu, la haine du
Christ, et j'ajouterai la haine de l'homme en tant qu'il a dignité et
indépendance et qu'il porte ainsi sur le visage un reflet de la
Divinité, la révolte bestiale contre tout principe de morale et
de spiritualité, c'est ce qui fait le caractère commun du bolchév-
isme et du nazisme, son succédané.

Et voici les paroles que le prophète met dans la bouche de
l'Agresseur: 'Je monterai vers la terre qui n'a pas de mur, j'irai
vers ces gens paisibles en pleine sécurité et qui n'ont murs ni
portes ni verrous à leur propriété. – Je m'adjugerai les dépouilles,
je confisquerai les biens, j'irai vers ce peuple qui occupe le milieu
de la terre.'

Mais Dieu prend à son tour la parole. Écoutez ce qu'il dit
à Jérémie: 'A mon tour je rendrai visite à Bel, et je lui ferai sortir
de la bouche ce qu'il avait absorbé, et les nations cesseront
d'avoir pente vers son gosier, car le mur de Babylone s'effondrera.
Sortez de lui, mon peuple!'

Et alors c'est le moment où interviennent les oiseaux. Quels
oiseaux, je vous le laisse à penser. Un ange frappe dans ses mains
et il convoque les oiseaux des quatre coins du ciel, disant: 'Hâtez-

vous! rassemblez-vous! Accourez de toutes parts vers la victime que je vous immole! une victime innombrable sur les montagnes d'Israël, afin que vous mangiez sa chair et que vous buviez son sang! Et le butin sera si énorme qu'il faudra 7 ans pour le recueillir!'

Qu'ajouter à ces paroles fatidiques? Mais si, il y a quelque chose à ajouter, et ce sont ces paroles qu'un poète a placées dans la bouche de Jeanne d'Arc et qui depuis que je les ai entendues à Bruxelles m'obsèdent comme un refrain:

Il y a l'espérance qui est la plus forte! il y a la foi qui est la plus forte! Il y a Dieu qui est le plus fort!

Paris le 13 Mars, 1940

12 · The Albums of Paul Claudel

JEAN MOUTON

PAUL CLAUDEL, at the end of his life, felt the need to create a form of television of his very own kind. He knew, better than anyone, the value of the pictorial image and its impact when cut out of its original context. Paul Claudel could not do otherwise than be his own impresario. Indeed he knew that we can do no more than *undergo* a picture which passes across a screen; we are incapable of stopping a moving sequence in order to isolate it, turn it over in our minds, and give it a new meaning. If there is movement, we are content to follow the movement. There is no possibility of going back and immobilizing what is under way. Nevertheless immobilization becomes at one point necessary, if we wish to allow the eye to be attentive, and to make comparisons.

A visionary like Claudel is not satisfied by the prefabricated image which is imposed on him, the image which he has no opportunity to re-create for himself. The image on the screen can never be thought out again, and Claudel will never be content to absorb what he has not prepared himself.

So what does he do? Two years before his death, he began to take all kinds of photographs out of newspapers and magazines. And, like a child, he stuck them into a series of albums. He collected the most anodine, most mediocre reproductions, which he could use as materials, and transformed them in his own imagination.

The first thing we find before us is naturally enough a collection of records of Claudel's public and private life: First Communions of his grandchildren, birthdays, gatherings in the big house at Brangues. One page shows us a monk stretched out in prayer for Paul Claudel. A special place is reserved for the faces of those who produced and performed his plays: Charles Dullin, Edwige Feuillère, J. L. Barrault, Madeleine Renaud. In the middle of a group of artists we see Ingrid Bergman; she is holding her hand on the poet's heart and declaring: 'Pourrais-je me trouver mieux?'

Another series of documents refer to certain events which have left their mark on the contemporary history of the Catholic Church. Pope Pius XII is many times presented to us: proclaiming the dogma of the Assumption, according an interview to the author of *L'Annonce faite à Marie*, participating at the consecration of Monsignor Montini as Archbishop of Milan, delivering an address in front of a radio microphone.

There are several pieces of testimony with regard to miracles. At Lourdes, we see a paralysed woman lifting her arm. Four young women are kneeling in a Church: the four seers of Beauraing. The miracle is not visibly marked here by the elements presented to us for observation. Considering Claudel's temperament this might be surprising; but he does not seem to be seeking what denotes the miraculous. Faced by these photographs, an observer who did not know about them would not be aware of the slightest trace of supernatural intervention.

These notebooks constitute at first an anthology of the poet's favourite painters, who had already filled the pages of *L'Oeil écoute*, but Claudel does not try to express himself about them, except on rare occasions. We find again the main lines of his choice. Firstly the visionaries, those who see beyond what we are shown by visible appearances – Hieronymus Bosch, Albrecht Dürer, Goya, Altdorfer – and who disturb our sense of balance by enclosing our view within an infinite projection of lines which cross and open out again every moment, everywhere around us, veritable abysses, as in Piranesi. On the other hand Rembrandt, who created the most vast and mysterious of worlds in painting, is also represented. Paul Claudel specially gave his attention to *Minerva*, *Saul and David* and, above all, *The Storm* (the commentary on it is not in the album itself), about which he stressed the fact that while the storms of poets and musicians pass those of painters do not; the painter has, in a sense, suspended time. The artist lets us participate in the joy that he felt in his composition, which expresses itself in this fine definition: 'Il faut qu'on sente le tableau jouir . . . de lui-même.'

The reproduction of the *Minerva* from the museum of The Hague includes a subtle analysis of all the elements contained in the picture: the goddess's shield which petrifies her enemies, the steel, the tortoise, two masks, pieces of cloth wound up on a chair; and all this collection of things harmonized by the alternations of darkness and light which make up the rhythm of the canvas itself. Again there is the *Saul and David* from the same museum, in which David is immersed in the poem he is composing on his harp in order to temper the infinite sadness of the king. This majestic sovereign is almost grotesque, with a tall and complicated turban on his head, surmounted by a derisory little crown, the same derisory little crown that Rembrandt places on the turbans of all tyrants. These tyrants are all very shortly going to be destroyed, like Saul, or like Balthazar in *The Feast* as he gazes at the mysterious hand writing the decree of his fate on the wall.

Other visionaries confide their torments to the wildness of water at night, as does Victor Hugo in *La Vague*, or let their eternal meditations reflect in calm, shimmering water, as does Vermeer.

Finally come those who devote themselves to light, sometimes a theatrical light marking the dramatic intensity surrounding one of the essential acts in the history of the world, as in Caravaggio's *Burial of Christ*; sometimes a light which gives fullness to forms and lets us hear, through their transparent solidity, a silent but urgent call, as in the *Nativity* of Georges de la Tour. Sometimes this light is reduced to the murky light of an oil lamp suspended from the smoky ceiling of a dark room, letting us divine the ungainliness of the human condition by the savage revelation it gives us of the way in which appetites, such as those in *The Potato Eaters* by Van Gogh, are satisfied.

The Vice-Roi in *Le Soulier de satin* does not hesitate to send Rubens a splendid statue of a woman, which an archaeologist has recently dug up: 'Je ne veux pas laisser ce prince des peintres tranquille au milieu de ses lys et de ses roses.' This is a challenge, not only aimed at animating the technical virtuosity of the recipient of the present, but also to arouse in him sensual emotion. The poet, too, is susceptible to such emotion; a collection of paintings brought together by Spanish kings seems to him 'un paradis de la chair'. We also find in one of the albums reproductions of Watteau and Renoir. For portraits of women in full gala dress, he knows that great painters feel the need to make their magnificent robes shimmer in broad surfaces; and so he turns to Ingres, who adds to the materials a suppleness and a radiancy that they seem to borrow from the skin of the models they cover.

Paul Claudel was particularly attached to Dutch and Flemish painting, for they have taken on the task of 'glorifying the present'. Thus the portraits of Franz Hals breathe the contentment of the moment; elsewhere, the abundance of foodstuffs in Jordaens' paintings give them the appearance of a friendly butcher's shop.

Finally, in opposition to all this, he searches out pure contemplatives like Vermeer, Chardin and Ricard (the portrait of Madame Arnavon); he feels attracted to Philippe de Champaigne, despite his Jansenism. He is especially arrested by the ex-voto composed on the occasion of the healing of Soeur Catherine de Sainte Suzanne, the daughter of the painter. There he finds that immobility which allows him most easily to breathe with the same spiritual breath, and the security which will make easier his retreat into his own inner being.

Paul Claudel also filled his album with many reproductions of portraits of writers, artists and famous men. Some are exhibited there like Saints in a reliquary: Rimbaud, the reading of whose *Illuminations* and *Saison en Enfer* gave him 'L'impression vivante et presque physique du surnaturel'; Baudelaire, whose collection *Mon Coeur mis à nu* overwhelmed him, making him conscious of the same anguishes and the same self-reproach. Beside Baudelaire's portrait he placed one of Jeanne Duval, thus pointing to a resemblance he believed he could see between the features of the lover and those of his mistress; with Jeanne gradually taking on the appearance of the face she had caused to suffer so much, as if a pair of torturing pincers gradually took on the form of the wrists they were destroying. Max Jacob, to whom he wrote in January 1937: 'Vous avez à la fois les dons d'un poète et les grâces d'un chrétien, et rien nulle part d'artificiel et de méchant, mais partout ces belles vertus qu'on appelle l'humilité et la charité, celle-ci dans son double sens.' Marie Noël is also among the poets he recognizes; and, naturally, Paul Verlaine, who so splendidly opens the collection of *Feuilles de Saints*, for he too has met Christ, 'l'homme étrange peu à peu qui devient mon Dieu et mon Seigneur'.

Then come the writers who have tried to examine the great mysteries, while remaining infinitely more aware of the shadows surrounding their approaches than of the possibility, however distant, of light; Kierkegaard and Kafka, whose *Prozess* seemed to him 'un des thèmes les plus riches et les plus poignants du drame humain, celui de la justice et de l'administration de la justice'.

There follows a series devoted to exceptional personalities: a genius like Einstein, heroes like Saint-Exupéry or Estienne d'Orves. One may wonder why Baron Haussmann is placed among them; but this was doubtless in order to give homage to the taste for order and for those monumental vistas which so attracted the poet. Did he not write of him: 'il a éveillé une cité qui éprouve le besoin de ranger à droite et à gauche pour donner champ au regard et place au sens'?

Once the saints and the heroes have been placed in their niches, the condemned are lined up and nailed to the pillory. Stendhal whom Claudel stigmatized in conversation as a 'froid simulateur' is at their head; and Ernest Renan, of whom he said that he had embarked on 'les bateaux qui échouent' is also represented. There are people whose role and whose destiny are an enigma to him: Anna Pauker, one of the leading figures in the Communist Party in Rumania, and the Abbé Massin, who in his time left the Church in a rather spectacular manner.

Finally there are those for whom he feels sympathy and even admiration, but whom he likes to smile at: George Sand, drawn by Alfred de Musset, and looking like a captivating intellectual girl; and further on, the old dowager of Nohant seems unable to resist being buried alive in a vast flounced dress.

But the most unusual aspect of these photographs cut out of newspapers, which reveal nothing at all unexpected about the poet's personality, but merely underline certain tendencies, is what could be called the search for the striking document.

First of all, various kinds of evidence of men's behaviour in public, whether they have been dragged out of their own personal pigeon-hole, or whether they never possessed one in the first place. The human being finds himself in these circumstances deprived of his humanity, reduced to the role of an object, as in the demonstration of Soviet Youth which we see before Lenin's mausoleum. Opposite the immense walls of the Kremlin a multitude of living bodies press together like insects, and the poet has written in the margin: 'N'est-ce pas un peu le décor de Jérôme Bosch?' By this statement is he not making it understood that there really is a temptation here of failing to recognize, or of fearing to recognize (if one has ever known it), what concerns the individual and what the mass? Christian thought strongly evokes the communal 'life to come'; it wants us to realize that community in this life. But it does not take away man's dignity, and everyone is still alone responsible for his acts. That is Baudelaire's wish: to be a Saint for oneself. On the other hand the temptation of the totalitarian community, where people as individuals do not exist, results in the negation of the human being; the single fact of knowing that one exists in God permits a true collective life. Other documents show us the negation of man, whether it be a view of the Warsaw ghetto, in which all the men present are living dead; or a scene, entitled 'Pompes funèbres à Shanghai', in which one can see a number of objects wrapped up in cloth sacks. These are bodies, transported on wheelbarrows in times of crisis.

In general, the poet's curiosity is directed towards what is disproportionate. Everything that is disproportionate (that is, beyond any possibility of harmony with man) grips him, like a call from a world other than our own.

Firstly, the mountain, in itself a symbol on earth of everything which goes beyond our capability of adaptation; the Jungfrau, Mont Blanc. The mountain is simply there, as Mallory replied to the man who asked him why he was trying to climb Everest. The mountain also brings us nearer to heaven: one photograph shows Hillary and Tensing on the summit of Everest, where they have just set up a flag. Paul Claudel has added this observation in ink: 'Il n'y a que le bouddhiste qui ait eu une pensée de reconnaissance vers le ciel.'

Finally, there is the mountain that kills, and, turning over a page, we see the summit of the Obiou, on which a plane full of Canadian pilgrims coming back from Rome crashed. The Obiou (in the Dauphiny Alps) is situated not far from La Salette, where two young shepherds saw a vision of the Virgin Mary. This death of a group of Christians, taking place between two places of Pilgrimage, might well have provoked Voltaire's smile about the efficacity of journeys guided by piety. But the Obiou disaster is there to remind us that earthly man remains a prey to all the forces which contribute to his life as well as to his destruction. The soul which has been brutally separated from the body can, according to Christian belief, immediately find itself in a state of eternity which will be a blessed eternity. For Paul Claudel, the plane-crash on these rocks at high altitude affirmed in some way the preparation of all these pilgrims to live 'de l'éternité'.

The writer's natural disposition to feel the impetus of the 'baroque', i.e. everything that moves, carries us away, or crushes us (as opposed to everything that immobilizes us, or reassures us), naturally induced him to collect monsters. The albums contain an impressive series of them: a mammoth, a Siberian fossil on whose strange form he comments thus: 'Que mangeait-il? L'éléphant consomme une tonne de matière végétale par jour', and he adds: 'Et ces défenses biscornues?' Then a giant octopus, whose motive system he describes. All of them are used to illustrate *La Légende de Prâkriti*, the text where he sets forth, with the prescience of a visionary, the commandments which God has made to 'la nature naturante', that nature which designates all the elements of the universe capable of replying to the Creator's invitation. Nature works with tremendous energy, and never ceases to provide; it sets about proposing models, working feverishly on the chosen data, not without some mistakes, but almost always with humour or even with mischievousness: 'Elle (la nature) rêve, elle bâille, elle dit oui, elle dit non, elle entend de travers, elle se livre à des calembours de sourde, à moins que ce ne soit de simples farces.' The Mammoth helps him to understand 'la nécessité des gros numéros et des gabarits imposants'; it belongs to the series of 'véritables tanks animaux'. Elsewhere it makes him think of 'des Tours de Babel ambulantes'. Faced by this phenomenon, it seems to him that 'Tout est à la fois disparate et exagération, un mélange de souvenirs et de prophéties, la matière pure qui essaye de montrer ce dont elle est capable et qui monte ces inspirations d'épopée et de blasphème, le premier beuglement autonome qui retentit dans l'atelier cosmique'.

As for the octopus, it evokes for him, as do birds and insects, Japanese warriors or those medieval warriors who 'proclament par un costume approprié, par ces armoiries sur la poitrine et par ce cimier emphatique, la place qu'ils tiennent dans la parade'. At the end of one album, an enormous bronze toad, serving as a heavy paperweight, occupies the final place, the place of honour; it reminds us of the poet's fellow feeling for this batrachian. In a kind of fellowship he discovers that as he, the ambassador, gets older, he comes more and more to resemble it; the decorations which an official envoy wears on his chest are reflected in the markings, amid the sheen of watered silk, on this hermit's back, who becomes increasingly pickled and paralysed: 'Il ne bouge pas, il pend et prie sur le dos et la tête en bas, il est accroché à une branche comme un fruit, comme un hamac, toute son existence est de rester là, de joindre les mains, non seulement les deux mains, mais les quatre pattes!'

*

The most perfect monster has been brought into being by man: the dislocated machine. The animal plays its role on earth, and its shape allots it to that role. Whether it dies a natural death or whether it is killed, it keeps, thanks to the protective magma provided by its flesh, a certain flexibility and even nobility; its dismembered corpse still indicates the logic of its construction. If it is crushed, its form is certainly rent; but then it disappears, reduced to a bloody little carpet, like a flattened ermine. But death in a car-accident is one of the most horrible there is; and Claudel, who had been cruelly hit by the death of his son-in-law, has isolated in these volumes some photographs of car accidents.

A car decaying in a field reaches the height of uselessness; its carcase destroys a landscape, for it does not mingle with the earth as easily as other forms of rubbish. A broken-down motor-car is a grotesque object. The solidity of its metal entrails makes it impossible for it to mingle with that sort of pulp from which living bodies originally came. Bits of smashed sheet-metal, pieces of broken glass resembling spear-heads, contorted pipes and bent shafts all intermingle like snakes. All this apparatus retains in death an appearance of cruelty, like subtle and complicated traps intended even more efficiently to break bodies. When two lorries crash these components which were given the appearance of solidity by their metal carapace, still display, when all their various parts have been scattered an air of permanence. The motor-car is an extreme example of that 'infatuation' which, according to Baudelaire, has been instilled in man by his idolatry of mechanical progress. Human industry behaves like nature which, having 'mis sur pied toute une ménagerie' suddenly gets tired of it: '. . . elle a mal au cœur, elle balaye le plateau d'un revers de bras et elle recommence, sur de nouveaux frais. Elle flanque au dépotoir des ordres entiers avec leurs genres, leurs sous-genres et leurs espèces, et ne garde qu'un pou et un criquet.' In these circumstances a steering-wheel on top of a pile of stones or a rubber tyre which has rolled into the grass, fits quite well into the category of 'ossements', to which he devotes a complete study under that name. As with the species of nature, an industrial construction is established when there is a vital need for it 'où l'erreur est payée de mort et où l'hésitation est interdite'. And he adds: 'Il faut que tout soit réalisé à la fois et d'un seul coup. Tout le monde sait les dégâts que le moindre vice de construction peut causer dans une automobile, un boulon desserré, un caprice de magnéto.'

There remains the greatest of all monstrosities: crime. Crime is the most disturbing sign of man's destiny; it reveals the fact that man remains continually exposed to the threat of vertigo. Crime reminds us that man, though he has been saved, is still capable of the most surprising falls. He is unstable; a colossus with feet of clay, whose whole structure is capable of crumbling. The creator of Mara knows, like Shakespeare, that evil exists, and that it manifests itself in a formidable positivity, This positivity, if it does not wash out the impurity of its source, justifies the account one takes of its action. Bibiane, who is the first version of Mara in *La Jeune Fille Violaine*, throws a handful of burning cinders into the eyes of her sister, whom she blinds. When, rendering good for evil, Violaine has by a miracle given back sight to Bibiane's blind child, she is struck down with stones by Bibiane. And of the Mara of *L'Annonce faite à Marie*, the sombre Mara contrasted with the heavenly light which surrounds her sister, Violaine says: 'Mara a toujours raison.' Is not Mara in fact, as Jacques Madaule says, 'la femme de la nécessité'? Is crime necessary, just as the damned man is necessary who 'éternellement brille de cette lumière qu'il repousse'?

The human being who takes up crime, or even only participates in it indirectly, is marked with a sign. Beside the photograph of the daughter of a man who was accused of a murder for which he was given a long prison sentence, a handwritten note by Claudel draws one's attention to the space between the young woman's eyes.

He collects the most diverse and antithetical types of criminal. Brute force, and an appetite for enjoyment and domination which will not diminish whatever the risk, are incarnated in an enormous body of vast breadth, like the base of a column capable of motion, which belongs to Goering, the caricature of the hero. Facing him, there is a picture of a crafty-looking, thin, prudent, calculating man. The sort of man who respects all the rules and customs, and takes politeness to an excessive degree of refinement. Beneath his bowler hat, that most common symbol of respectability, we recognize Landru, his slightly slit eyes betraying a determination as recognizable as it is veiled. This murderer of a very large, if indeterminate, number of women represents a kind of anti-hero, but the caricature of an anti-hero (the true anti-hero certainly commits evil and treacherous acts, but in a climate of open, not suppressed, violence). This modern Bluebeard, by his sense of economization of means, and by the silence (one might almost say moderation) with which he accomplishes his deeds, comes rather from a kind of classical tradition.

We begin to understand the constant link between hypocrisy and crime; hypocrisy the offensive arm which prepares the crime; hypocrisy the defensive arm which protects the man who has carried it out. This fact leads us to define the only true hypocrisy, that which consists of masking an evil action behind the name of God. This is the most wicked form of hypocrisy; and perhaps there is no other kind. Tartuffe is certainly the true hypocrite, but he is doubtless the only one. Hypocrisy gives to the man who uses it a terrible weapon; and inversely, the very word 'hypocrisy', which in itself contains no more danger than an empty scabbard, can end up by constituting a very real peril through the improper use that is made of it. Those who are themselves inclined to be hypocritical are the first to apply the name to everything they particularly want to destroy. Stendhal had a strong predilection for mathematics because it is neither hypocritical nor vague, and yet the day came when he almost doubted its sincerity; now, the creator of Julien Sorel showed himself to be one of the people most inclined to flavour everything which ran counter to his ideological *parti pris* with this suspicion of hypocrisy. Everything can become hypocrisy: the nuances of thought, that poetry which transforms the world, delicacy of feeling, everything which is not clear-cut and systematic, everything which cannot conform to the rules of what are today called 'structures'.

We already know of Paul Claudel's lack of sympathy (that is the least one can say) for Stendhal, who according to him, had put on every possible mask. In fact Stendhal, could not prevent himself from putting the same masks on all the faces symbolizing what he detested. In this way he was no longer forced to recognize them.

These albums present us with true hypocrisy in both its forms. First of all hypocrisy as a defensive weapon is represented by Marie Besnard, who was accused of several poisonings, bowing beneath the magical effect of her black clothes. Her face is puckered up; she does not try to justify what she is said to have done by hiding behind the name of God, but she uses what St Rose of Lima calls the greatest gift that God has ever given us: tears. As we look at her face as she tries to hide it behind her hands, these tears seem to us uncertain in import. Is it the terror of innocence which knows that it will never be able to get out of the trap into which unjust suspicions have made it fall? Is it a feeling of self-pity which leaves out of account crimes which have in fact been committed? Is she weeping for herself, as if the others were betraying her merely by accusing her?

Hypocrisy also becomes an offensive weapon. To prove it the poet has not cut out a photograph but, what is a much rarer thing in his albums, a newspaper article. In this case, it consists of two columns by Morvan Lebesque under the title of 'Némésis à Kansas'. The article summarizes the story of a crime committed by a couple in Kansas City in 1953. A man and a woman kidnapped a six-year-old boy called Bobby Greenlease, the son of a rich car merchant. The ransom demanded was 500,000 dollars, a fantastic sum, but the father had decided to hand it over in compliance with the kidnappers' instructions; and this was in fact done. One of the instructions was that the ransom should be paid in one-dollar bills in order to facilitate disposal. So several suitcases filled with banknotes were placed one evening near a railway bridge, the place fixed for the rendezvous. The suitcases were taken away, but the child was not given back. In fact the two criminals were murderers who had killed the child one hour after the kidnapping. But what had attracted Paul Claudel's attention was the way in which the kidnapping was carried out. The child was a pupil at a religious college in Kansas City, One morning, a woman had turned up saying that young Bobby Greenlease's mother was ill and that he was to be taken to see her immediately. Paul Claudel wrote in the margin beside the article this formidable annotation: 'La femme de l'assassin était venue chercher l'enfant à l'école catholique en se donnant pour sa tante. Elle était restée quelque temps en prière dans la chapelle'. A perfect Tartuffe, dressed in his black cloak, thus led a young child to his death.

Paul Claudel sometimes gives himself up to phantasy, like a child who, in the middle of its greatest activity, is able for an instant (sometimes for a few seconds) to suspend time; he looks at things with his whole body and what he sees becomes miraculous. This sudden halt in the writer's work, this pause devoted to distraction, allows him to immobilize the movement of beings and things. The moment that is thus fixed in time gives us some surprising sights, such as the little girl looking at herself in a sloping looking-glass whose mouth drops open in amazement as she sees herself in this way, and our mouths drop open with hers. Elsewhere, a child stretched out on a patch of grass, his head in his hands, seems to be sleeping. To wake him up, someone, of whom one can only see the hand (as in certain representations of God in the primitives), is throwing a bucket of water over him. The liquid content is coming out of the receptacle in a wide surface, like a great concave leaf whose exterior veins are beginning to detach themselves in little, diamond-like drops: and the immobility of the picture transforms them into little luminous globes, gently descending.

These albums filled with 'collages' fulfilled several roles for the poet as he felt the approach of death: a recapitulation of family memories, a chance to look again at the great manifestations of a life engaged in a living Christian faith; but also, and above all, the preservation of the essence of that which had animated his passions. As he entered little by little the corridors which led him to the antechamber of death, he collected these photographs torn out of newspapers with a kind of feverishness. Like little signs which could show him, and others, the road to follow, he places them, like landmarks, on these dark walls, which are for a moment illuminated by them.

Part three · Claudel and England

13 · Claudel, Patmore and Alice Meynell: some contacts with English Catholicism

PATRICK MCCARTHY

IT IS IMPOSSIBLE in an article of this length to deal fully with the influence of English Catholic writers on Paul Claudel, or with the reception of his work in English circles. One aspect alone – although a two-sided aspect – can be treated here: the publication of Claudel's translations of Coventry Patmore in the *Nouvelle Revue Française* in 1911 and the impact of *L'Otage* on Alice Meynell. The two are interrelated since it was through the Patmore translation that Alice Meynell came into contact with Claudel, via Valery Larbaud who was, as so often, a link between England and France and was also personally involved in the debate about Catholicism. And if this contact is only one of many in Claudel's surprisingly varied career as a writer it still reveals the complex background of the *NRF* interest in Catholicism and in English Catholics and spotlights one particular attitude that is common to Claudel, Patmore and Alice Meynell.

For Claudel's translations of G. K. Chesterton and of Patmore are only part of the general *NRF* preoccupation. Now around 1910 there is in the *NRF* an atmosphere of conversion, or perhaps of pre-conversion, which expresses itself differently in each of the writers, but which constitutes an important trend in the review. Claudel stands at the centre of the various problems and entanglements as the champion of Catholicism, and the most important issue is, of course, the possible conversion of Gide. Having failed once, in 1905, Claudel was wary now, but Gide seemed to dangle the prospect of his conversion in front of him. The death of Charles-Louis Philippe in December 1909 revived the discussion, because Gide insisted that Philippe was on the verge of conversion when he died. Claudel did not agree, and neither did Philippe's friends, but Gide was using Philippe's conversion as a pretext for talking about his own, while at the same time he resisted Claudel's influence in his *Journal* – a subtle and characteristically Gidean kind of sincerity. At the same time Claudel was making a more open effort to win over the young Jacques Rivière, whose fierce intellectual and emotional need for certainty was to bring him to conversion at the end of 1913. Valery Larbaud was received into the Catholic Church in December 1910 – one year to the day after the funeral of Philippe – but he did not reveal this to anyone until early 1912 when he confided in Gide. Since Gide was also of Protestant background and influenced by an over-dominant mother he was an eminently suitable confidant, except that he promptly informed Claudel – much to Larbaud's annoyance, for his Catholicism in no way measured up to Claudel's. But here again Gide wished to present Claudel with a conversion in order to hint at his own. Meanwhile on the outskirts of this activity hovered Francis Jammes, partially estranged from Gide but another confidant for Larbaud who found his version of Catholicism less severe than Claudel's.[1]

So the *NRF* milieu around 1911 was a veritable hive of influences, resistance to influences, conversions and possible conversions. In this Claudel is the one man whose position is fixed: while Gide and Larbaud oscillate, advance and withdraw, Claudel's letters to them are full of certainty. Moreover, there is no room for compromise in Claudel's world and he insists on the difficult aspects of Catholicism. As early as 1907 he warns Rivière: 'Il y a bien des choses qui vous paraissent infiniment douces ou terriblement désirables, auxquelles vous avez à renoncer. Et d'autre part dans la religion catholique il y a tant de choses dures à croire, tant de choses humiliantes à pratiquer!'[2] It was Claudel's proselytizing fervour and the strictness of his doctrine that made him feared at the *NRF*. When he moved to Frankfurt in September 1911 he invited Gide and Larbaud to come and visit him, but neither of them ever went. Indeed they seem at this time to form a common front against him, discussing their problems together, writing to him but discreetly avoiding him. Gide feared perhaps that Claudel might not appreciate his complex kind of sincerity, and Larbaud that Claudel might detect some contradiction between his spiritual fervour and lax morality.

Now the translations and studies of English Catholics that appear in the *NRF* around this time are closely related to the debate that goes on within the group. Larbaud's study of Patmore and his pieces on Francis Thompson contain many of the themes present in his own conversion. Similarly Claudel's translation from Chesterton's *Orthodoxy* (1910)[3] seems almost to be a deliberate attempt to refute the picture of orthodoxy given in Gide's *Le Retour de l'Enfant Prodigue*. In place of the picture of Catholicism as a return to order where the best elements in the self are neglected, Claudel stresses that life for the Catholic is joyful and exciting. Orthodox christianity does not reside 'dans une certaine neutralité médiocre, mais dans des sentiments d'apparence contradictoire poussés à leur degré extrême d'intensité'.[4] Claudel was interested in other English Catholics apart from Chesterton – who was, of course, an Anglican at this time. He was one of the very few French writers to take up Newman, and after the war he published translations from Francis Thompson. Both Claudel and Larbaud wished to see in England a revival of idealist literature concerned with spiritual values, and a Catholicism based on adventure and not mere submission to an outside order. When Claudel writes of Coventry Patmore that 'si l'on songe à l'époque stupide ou il ecrivait, C.P. . . . a été le plus étonnant des initiateurs',[5] he is setting up Patmore as the forerunner of a new kind of literature that is akin to the reaction in France against the generation of Taine and the Naturalists.

For it is this kind of exuberant Catholicism that Claudel finds in Patmore, whom he discovered in 1900 and read and translated intermittently over the next ten years. Gabriel Frizeau was quick to see the affinities with Claudel himself: 'il est catholique comme vous nous avez appris à l'être',[6] he writes of Patmore. Central to Patmore, as to Claudel, is the notion of human love as foreshadowing the love of God, and the whole of his work and religion are based on a great emotional upsurge.

Now the Claudel–Patmore question has been carefully studied

by M. Guyard[7] who concludes that the core of Claudel's attraction to Patmore is the notion of the 'fini' that he sees everywhere in the *Unknown Eros*. Claudel calls it 'la doctrine de la *fermeture*, de la fin, de l'inépuisable dans l'éternellement formé'.[8] It sets out that human emotions must be disciplined so that they may take their place in the divine scheme of things; in particular love cannot be allowed to pursue its course unchecked, but must be channelled so that it may become a preparation for divine love. M. Guyard's interpretation is certainly correct and it receives additional support from a hitherto unpublished letter from Claudel to Alice Meynell given later in this study. It remains only to add that Claudel is right in insisting on this aspect of Patmore. Professor J. C. Reid, the best of recent critics of Patmore,[9] similarly stresses the role of law in his work, and points out that it is the desire for law that makes Patmore the poet of conjugal love. *Legem Tuam Dilexi* protests against the 'horrible' word of the infinite and against the 'bond-disdaining spirit', God, claims Patmore, is 'full of bonds'![10]. Both Claudel and Patmore are opposed to Romantic love where the lover's unsatisfied emotions spill out endlessly in defiance of limits. There is a strong ascetic strain in Patmore that leads him to dwell on the value of pain – 'Choice food of sanctity'.[11] Man's love is purified by pain and renunciation so that it may attain God. Patmore's dictum: 'Refuse it, Mortal, that it may be yours'[12] sums up the theme of *Partage de midi* where Mesa and Ysé must be maimed and burned before they can come together in the fullness of their love. Claudel sees in Patmore a man fearful like himself of 'the ghastly boundlessness' of space.[13]

Now the insistence on law does not – in either Patmore or Claudel – contradict the notion that religion is an adventure. Indeed it is the dialogue between the emotion and the law that constitutes the drama of Christian life – the drama that Claudel persistently opposes to Gide's view of orthodoxy as dull submission. But Claudel's desire to see law in Patmore does tie up with his position at the *NRF* as the champion of a strict Catholicism.

It also led him to a minor but characteristic dispute with Valery

Larbaud. Larbaud wrote the introductory study to Claudel's translation and he was by 1911 deeply involved with English Catholicism. Like Claudel, Larbaud was looking in England for a religion that was not merely a 'retour' – to order, to the family and to the land. He saw English Catholicism as a reaction against Victorian puritanism. But, unlike Claudel, Larbaud was not concerned with asceticism and in his study of Patmore he lays great stress on the role of human love in guiding Patmore to Catholicism, and correspondingly less stress on the need to discipline this love.[14] There was an amusing flurry of correspondence about this, for Claudel was displeased by Larbaud's use of the expression 'l'instinct sexuel' to describe Patmore's conversion motives. He explained himself in his usual forthright way, and stated his preference for the phrase 'l'instinct sacramentel' which, of course implies the need for spiritual law. Larbaud's replies are characteristically evasive although he does not dare to argue.[15] A small difference of opinion, but the mark of a wide gulf between Larbaud and Claudel.

By 1911 Larbaud had also made the acquaintance of Alice Meynell. Now she had been a close friend of Patmore during his later years, and she and her husband, Wilfrid Meynell, had been the protectors of Francis Thompson. By 1911 the Meynell circle was shrinking, their family was growing up and Wilfrid Meynell had many interests that were not Larbaud's. But their house was still a centre of Catholic life and their Sunday evenings were well attended. To these came Larbaud, introduced by a friend of the family, Daniel O'Connor. He talked with Alice Meynell and she encouraged his interest in Patmore and Thompson, while he told her about Claudel.

Although Larbaud gave a kind review to Alice Meynell's *Poems* in 1913, neither he nor Claudel was really interested in her work. Yet she exemplifies in many of her poems and essays the kind of joyful Catholicism that they were looking for. She was a lover of Italy and essays like *Ceres Runaway* express all the joy of Southern Europe opposed to the gloomy North; she was a foe of Victorian prudery and *Northern Fancy* extolls the virtues of the seventeenth century – its vigour and intense spirituality – over and above her own age, She was well placed to appreciate Patmore's poetry for her own poem *To the Body*, although quite different in style, expresses the same view of physical life as the Patmore poem of that title: the body is not tied to this world but awaits 'the appeal of God'.[16] She was keenly aware, too, of the ascetic strain in Patmore and expresses it in *Mr Coventry Patmore's Odes*, although she sees it in stylistic terms. She contrasts Patmore's usual grandiose style and luxuriant images with the moments when his poetry attains 'silence'[17] – a naked simplicity of language shorn of all ostentation. Alice Meynell admires this silence which is, after all, the stylistic expression of the concern for self-limitation that attracts Claudel.

She also sided with Claudel in disliking Larbaud's emphasis on sexual love in Patmore.[18] Whereas Larbaud wants to show how close Patmore's religion lay to human love, Alice Meynell and Claudel see the spiritual as a separate realm and demand that the physical be transformed in order to enter it. Alice Meynell followed Claudel's translations with interest: she suggested minor alterations and sent him a copy of her essay on Patmore. Her enthusiasm pleased Claudel and after the publication of the poems in book form he sent her a long letter postmarked 5 December 1912:

Francfort sur le Main

Je savais par Larbaud les liens d'amitié qui vous unissaient avec le grand poëte Coventry Patmore et votre appréciation de la traduction que j'ai tentée de quelques unes de ses œuvres m'est bien précieuse. Vous savez qu'on m'a reproché un manque parfois de fidélité littérale, mais j'ai traduit CP comme je voudrais être traduit moi-même, moins par le dictionnaire que par le cœur, en contemplant longuement le texte, en le repensant mot à mot, en recréant les mêmes pensées et en essayant de les rendre ensuite par les mots d'une autre langue. Vous conviendrez que ce n'est pas une petite affaire de *transsubstantier* un pareil poëte! Je sais que les quelques échantillons que j'ai donnés de sa poésie ne sont pas suffisants pour le faire juger mais si j'avais voulu traduire tout l'*Eros*, ma vie n'y aurait pas suffi.

C'est Algar Thorold (un ecrivain que vous connaissez peut-être) qui autrefois m'a fait lire CP au monastère maintenant désert de Solesmes, et depuis, le petit livre vert ne m'a pas quitté dans tous mes voyages. Il n'y a jamais eu de penseur plus neuf, plus audacieux que CP (en même temps que de plus grand artiste) et qui ait plus fait pour ouvrir enfin à l'Art les immenses domaines de la Religion. C'est lui qui en face de l'univers infini, indéfini, indéterminé et chaotique sur lequel les poëtes du XIX siècle ont fait tant de rhétorique, a rétabli pour la première fois l'idée de ce monde *fini* et parfait, dont son Créateur lui-même a dit qu'il le trouvait *très-bon*. C'est lui qui a montré la profonde homogénéité de tous les sentiments humains, même de ceux qui reçoivent si facilement une forme coupable, avec ceux dont un cœur religieux seul fournit l'expression parfaite, et qui a par ainsi montré la valeur suprême d'un art *catholique*, c-a-d vraiment universel, hors duquel la nature humaine reste insatisfaite et inarticulée (oui, malgré les plus beaux *cris*!).

Me trouverez – vous bien vaniteux, si je dis que la sympathie qu'ont rencontrée mes œuvres auprès de vous me touche profondément? J'aime tant la littérature anglaise, la première du monde par certains côtés, et cependant je n'avais jusqu'ici reçu de votre pays aucune marque d'appréciation.

Veuillez agréer, chère madame, mes respectueux hommages
P.C.[19]

This letter contains little that Claudel has not expressed elsewhere and that is not already known, but it is a good résumé of his long preoccupation with Patmore. Alice Meynell's praise of his translations was all the more welcome because they had been criticized, and the attack he refers to here was made by Henry D. Davray, the English critic of the *Mercure de France*. Davray did not always view the rival *Nouvelle Revue Française* with a kindly eye, and while he praised Larbaud's study of Patmore he disliked Claudel's translations. Larbaud made a rather ineffectual reply on Claudel's behalf, affirming that Patmore's son thought the translations were good,[20] but the best reply is made by Claudel here: the statement of his practice as a translator.

Claudel repeats here that it was Algar Thorold who told him of Patmore at Solesmes monastery in 1900. Thorold was the son of the Anglican bishop of Rochester and Winchester and, like so many others of his generation, he was converted to Catholicism. He was received into the Catholic Church in 1884, the year in which he went up to Oxford. He later spent much time at the Grande Chartreuse and considered entering the priesthood. He was interested in mysticism, and had already before 1900 published a book on the subject and done a translation of Catherine of Sienna. So it is neither surprising that he should have admired Patmore nor that he should have had much to talk about with a Claudel who was himself considering the priesthood. Claudel made vague inquiries about Thorold at this time – around 1911–12 – but they were of no avail. Thorold was now working on his monumental biography of his uncle, Henry Labouchere, which reveals another side of his character – the worldly, sceptical side – and was perhaps less preoccupied with religion. He later regained his enthusiasm and from 1926–34 was the editor of the *Dublin Review*, but he seems to have had no further contact with Claudel.

In his remarks about Patmore's poetry in the letter, Claudel insists once again on Patmore's role as the innovator of a new religious literature, on the concept of the finite, ordered world as opposed to the limitless, Kantian world of the late nineteenth century, and on the theme of love as a potential spiritual force.

When he comes to discuss his own work Claudel is clearly flattered by Alice Meynell's interest and he expresses elsewhere – in a letter to Larbaud [21] – his disappointment that no attention had been paid to him in England until now. Now Larbaud had not presented Claudel to the Meynells simply as the translator of Patmore. Larbaud regarded himself as an ambassador for the kind of French literature he admired – Claudel, Gide, Jammes and Philippe. He read Claudel's *Odes* at Alice Meynell's house and introduced her to the plays, especially to *L'Otage* of which he was a particular admirer. Now the Meynell circle was very willing to be interested in French Catholic writing which it saw as a new and encouraging trend. Larbaud describes this attitude to Claudel: 'Mrs Meynell avait jusqu'ici un certain préjugé contre les lettres françaises contemporainesl Son approbation vous vaut trente ou quarante lecteurs ici, dans un milieu . . . qui condamnait en bloc toute la littérature des vingt dernières années comme agnostique, immorale et inartistique.'[22] As Larbaud and Claudel were anxious to see a Catholic revival in England so the Meynell circle followed the revival in France – a friend of Alice Meynell called Agnes Tobin was an ardent admirer of Jammes. Alice Meynell was taken by *L'Otage* and wished to translate it. There were difficulties about the translation rights – the correspondence about this reveals Claudel's eagerness to be translated by her and also the *NRF's* willingness to do almost anything to please Claudel[23] – and finally she published a study of the play with long quotations translated by herself in the *Dublin Review* 1918.

Claudel's work has never been terribly popular in England, not even in Catholic circles, and *L'Otage* is peculiarly French in its debate about the value of the 'terre', so Alice Meynell's deep interest in the play must spring from a personal source, over and above the part played by Larbaud as a link and her natural interest in French Catholicism. It is the figure of Sygne, the woman from whom is demanded the impossible, who is called upon to make a sacrifice that no one can measure or appreciate around her, who attracts Alice Meynell.

For perhaps the deepest strain in her work is the sense of privacy and the need for renunciation. In her most joyful moments she is conscious that each individual is separate from all others, like the mountains covered with the first snows of Winter that 'keep their counsel sealed and fast'.[24] In *A Poet's Wife* the poet remains detached even when locked in his wife's embrace, and in *The Unknown God* Christ descends at communion into the man seated next to the poet, but He remains enclosed with 'this lonely conscience'.[25] There is not in Alice Meynell the agonizing sense of man shut off permanently from other men, much less from God, for this same poem ends with a confident appeal to Christ. But she does feel that man must work out his salvation alone, and that the innermost recesses of the human personality cannot be invaded from outside.

Linked with this is an ascetic strain: a liking for self-discipline and an aesthetic distrust of the ostentatious. Now this runs peculiarly close to the theme of joy, for Alice Meynell sees her beloved Italian landscapes as hard and sinewy whereas the English countryside is 'fat'.[26] Renunciation is seen as a condition of striving, and Alice Meynell seeks out the limits that man imposes on himself. Particularly relevant here is the poem *Renouncement* (meant for Coventry Patmore?) where the poetess withdraws from any guilty love with the simple watchword: 'I must not think of thee'.[27] This desire for law – the willingness to accept limits as the price and condition of the spiritual – makes a special link between Claudel, Patmore and Alice Meynell that goes beyond the general recognition that they are all writers trying to forge a Catholic literature.

It is the sense of a spiritual struggle carried on in isolation and demanding abnegation that Alice Meynell recognizes in Sygne. After reading the play she wrote to Larbaud to thank him for making Claudel's work known to her, and she describes *L'Otage* as the 'most tragic tragedy I have ever known, because of its great spirituality'.[28] The particular way that she links the tragic and the spiritual becomes apparent in her 1918 study.

She chooses to translate long extracts from the scene between Sygne and Badilon in Act II, where Sygne submits and accepts that she must marry Turelure, and the scene between Sygne and Georges in Act III, where Georges does not submit and tries to kill Turelure. The significance of these scenes and of the play lies, for Alice Meynell, in the extent of Sygne's abnegation. When she calls *L'Otage* 'a tragedy as *Lear* is not and *Othello* is not'[29] she means that in *Othello* something has been saved: by the time that Othello commits suicide he knows that Desdemona was innocent so that posthumously her honour is saved. For Sygne nothing is saved: her abnegation has produced – so it seems at least – no gain and

Georges will not recognize it. Contrasting *Othello* and *L'Otage*
Alice Meynell writes: 'Honour is a noble thing of this world . . .
M. Claudel seems resolved to take the woman of his play, and the
audience, into higher places.'[30] This is a reasoned development of
her original remark to Larbaud: the spiritual is tragic because it
can be achieved only at the cost of everything prized in this world.
Sygne as a woman is destroyed and leaves behind her no memory
of honour. The spiritual is linked with a dimension of abnegation
that is, in Alice Meynell's opinion, new and peculiar to Claudel
and it is this abnegation, made freely and in the most total solitude,
that appeals to Alice Meynell.

Yet she too wonders whether Claudel might not have asked too
much of his heroine. Now this is a criticism that occurs naturally
to the ordinary reader, but Alice Meynell's point of view is rather
exceptional and in harmony with her other remarks about the
play. She does not think that Sygne should have been allowed to
follow the natural course of her love for Georges. Such a criticism
would imply as a premise the right of the individual to love freely.
Alice Meynell's criticism is anti-individualist: she wonders
whether Sygne has the right to marry Turelure because it means
giving birth to a child who would inherit the evil characteristics
of his father. The really unhappy figure in the play is thus Sygne's
child who has been brought into life with a natural inclination
towards evil. Alice Meynell asks: 'Is a woman to bear an heir to
an habitual assassin's heart, to an habitual traitor's brain, in order
to save her country?'[31] Of course in making this criticism Alice
Meynell is ignoring the Claudelian sense of the divine purpose
running through history that is one of the main themes of the
trilogy: Turelure's child is a necessary part in the scheme of
things, and the full unrolling of the scheme is revealed only in *Le
Père humilié*. In giving birth to her child Sygne is expressing confidence in God's plan. But more important here is to examine
Alice Meynell's standpoint: it is deliberately anti-romantic. She
puts forward a view of marriage as governed not by personal
wishes, but by the remembrance that the choice of a lover is also
the choice of a father for the child. This is a view that emphasizes

renunciation of self just as surely as does the Claudelian insistence on acquiescence into the divine plan.

So the meetings between Valery Larbaud and Alice Meynell proved as fruitful to Paul Claudel as his own meetings some years earlier with Algar Thorold. These are two of the rare examples of contact between the Catholic Revivals in England and France and interesting in themselves as such. But they also reflect Claudel's position in the thought of the period and particularly in the *NRF* milieu: his desire to offer examples of a Catholicism that is dynamic and exciting and that also stresses the need for discipline. Then out of this springs the connection and interraction among Claudel, Patmore and Alice Meynell: in all three of them is the sense that the spiritual is indeed a development of the human, but that limits must be set – a view that separates them, for example, from Larbaud. This is too the first time that Claudel's work aroused sympathy in England. Alice Meynell's study of *L'Otage* remains a lonely landmark, for English Catholics have not followed her. It is regrettable that they have been so hesitant after this interesting first step towards an understanding of Claudel's work.

NOTES

1. For much information about the *NRF* I am indebted to M. Auguste Anglès who has kindly allowed me to read his yet unpublished thesis 'La Nouvelle Revue Française, 1908–14'.

2. *Jacques Rivière et Paul Claudel. Correspondance, 1907–14*, Paris: Plon, 1949, p. 23.

3. G. K. Chesterton, *Les Paradoxes du Christianisme*, Traduction de Paul Claudel, *NRF*, t. 4, pp. 129–64.

4. *Jacques Rivière et Paul Claudel. Correspondance, 1907–14*, p. 187.

5. Paul Claudel to Valery Larbaud, 11.10.1911. Quoted by G. Jean-Aubry, *Valery Larbaud: sa vie et son oeuvre*, Monaco: Edition du Rocher, 1949.

6. P. *Claudel*, F. *Jammes*, G. *Frizeau. Correspondance, 1897–1938*, Paris: Gallimard, 1952, p. 80.

7. Marius-François Guyard, *De l'Eros Inconnu aux Grandes Odes. Bibliothèque Française et romaine*, Serie C.VI, published by Centre de Philologie romane de la Faculté des lettres de Strasbourg, 1963, pp. 75–107.

8. *Paul Claudel et André Gide. Correspondance, 1899–1926*, Paris: Gallimard, 1949, p. 125.

9. J. C. Reid, *The Mind and Art of Coventry Patmore*, London: Routledge, 1957, pp. 125 f.

10. *The Poems of Coventry Patmore*, London: O.U.P. ,1949 ed., pp. 405–6.

11. ibid., p. 434.

12. ibid., p. 394.

13. ibid., p. 405.

14. *NRF.*, t. V, pp. 273–97, and pp. 398–419. Reproduced in *Œuvres complètes III*, pp. 58–106.

15. Paul Claudel to Valery Larbaud, 11.10.1911, and Valery Larbaud to Paul Claudel, 17.11.1911. Quoted by G. Jean-Aubry, op. cit., pp. 185, 188.

16. *The Poems of Alice Meynell*, Centenary Ed., London: Hollis and Carter, 1947, p. 60.

17. Alice Meynell, *The Rhythm of Life and Other Essays*, London: Matthews & Lane, 1893, p. 90.

18. Valery Larbaud to Paul Claudel, 17.11.1911. Quoted by Jean-Aubry, op. cit., p. 188.

19. I wish to express my gratitude to Mrs. O. Sowerby for permission to reproduce this letter (which I have just learnt has also appeared as part of an article by L.-A. Colliard entitled 'Claudel traducteur de Patmore', *Estratto Da: Culture Française*, Bari: Anno XIV, no. 6, 1967) and to Miss Genevieve Hawkins for drawing my attention to it. This letter and the two letters referred to in reference 23 are in the possession of Mrs Sowerby.

20. Paul Claudel to Valery Larbaud, 19.7.1911. Quoted by Jean-Aubry, op. cit., p. 179.

21. *Mercure de France*, XCIV (1.12.1911), p. 667.

22. Valery Larbaud to Paul Claudel, 14.7.1911. Quoted by Jean-Aubry, op. cit., p. 178.

23. Paul Claudel to Alice Meynell, 5.1.1917, and *NRF* to Alice Meynell, 30.1.1917.

24. *The Poems of Alice Meynell*, p. 57.

25. ibid., p. 49.

26. *The Rhythm of Life and Other Essays*, p. 83.

27. *The Poems of Alice Meynell*, p. 13.

28. Alice Meynell to Valery Larbaud (undated). Bibliothèque Municipale Vichy.

29. Alice Meynell, '*L'Otage* of Paul Claudel', *Dublin Review*, 163 (July/Aug./Sept., 1918), p. 58.

30. ibid.

31. ibid., p. 59.

14 · Meditation on a text by Claudel

ALEXANDER MAVROCORDATO

(To a Lady Who Always Does the Wrong Thing)

THERE IS NOTHING more touching than the sight of a great poet at grips with a language which is not his own. We feel he is wooing an elusive mistress who lends him her body, rather than gives him her soul. An aura of mystery surrounds her. The pleasure she bestows grants him no rights, nor her weakness any power over her person. The tighter he clasps her, the more she escapes him.

We receive an impression of this sort from Claudel's *The Lady Who Always Did the Right Thing*, a prose-poem published in an American review[1] at a time when the French poet was still ambassador in Washington. It is cast in the form of a parable, a kind he had already used to bring home to us, through the story of *Animus and Anima*[2], Rimbaud's terrible secret. It is not widely known, so let us read it over again.

THE LADY WHO ALWAYS DID THE RIGHT THING
A Story

A Very Fine and Refined Lady saw herself in a dream, as, just like the Hercules between two roads, she stood at the entrance of a theatre or Music-Hall. The passage on her left was a narrow steep and rather dirty staircase, lighted by raw and vulgar gas-jets, no doubt leading to the Upper Circle, what is called in French 'Paradis'. The other passage at right hand was a wide, spacious and dignified porch, with thick carpets, tapestries, gracious statues and interesting pictures, gently sloping to the correct level. All well dressed people, ladies and gentlemen, all people who are counting for something, were going this way, amiably laughing, chattering and chafing each other, all ready to enjoy themselves to the utmost and to have a good time. Of course our very Fine and Refined Lady had not the least shadow of a hesitation to go the same way. Oily and smiling Ushers came to meet all those charming people and verified their tickets. The Refined Lady showed hers, who was not of the same colour as the others, but the Ushers made no remarks and introduced her with a respectful bow.

Well! after all it was not a Theatre or Music-Hall, rather it was a kind of enormous Waiting room, or, strange as it may appear, a Justice Court, like the Midnight Court in New York. Thousands and thousands of men and women were there, all silent or talking quietly to each other. The Refined Lady looked through her 'face-à-main' and was simply delighted to see there all of her friends, enemies and acquaintances, all having a rather subdued appearance. In fact they did not answer or only a few muttered words as she gaily made inquiries and tried to find her own seat. Many people also were there whom she had not seen from a very long time. How jolly and pleasant! But no, it was not jolly and pleasant at all. On the contrary there was everywhere a kind of dark and constrained expression, as if everybody was suffering under some undeserved infliction. On the other side of the enormous Room, as far as you could see, were all kinds of impossible people, of loathsome and vulgar customers, all boisterous and mirthful and slightly intoxicated. The Refined Lady wondered how they received admittance anyhow, and why they looked so pleased as her own neighbours looked stiff, silent, subtly hurt, decorously pained and congealed in a condition of injured dignity. The Refined Lady felt herself ill at ease and out of place in that grim judicial Apartment, the more so as the numbers on her ticket were very confusing and she could not succeed in finding her seat.

At that moment she heard one of the Ushers, or was it a police man, like a page in the hall of an hotel, bawling her name. 'Here I am, Sir!' she shouted. 'Yes, Sir, I am Madame So and So.' The Usher took her ticket and looked surprised. 'Well, Madame, I just looked for you everywhere, but may I ask you how you are sitting at the *left* side of His Lordship when you were expected at His *right*?' 'I don't know who is that Lordship of whom you are speaking. Is it not here a Theatre which was made for the enjoyment of the playgoers? As I stood in the entrance, I saw two passages, one at my left, and the other at my right, and of course I took the right one. I was always instructed to do the Right Thing. Do the Right Thing, as always told me my dear mother, and in the long run you will find it also the easiest and the most convenient. It will pay you to do Right. I always did and found no difficulty. It is not difficult for a right nature to do the right thing. I think I can be no wrong if I always take the right side, if I insist on my Right, if I follow with an unwavering confidence what was written for all times in the immortal Declaration of Rights.' And the Usher said: 'Don't you see the colour of your ticket? The fact is that you are not now at the Right of His Lordship, but at His Left. By always doing what seemed you right, by always taking the right side, by always following with a full confidence your inner Declaration of Rights, the . . . fact is that you did not arrive at the Right Side of His Lordship, but at His Left.' 'Well,' said the Refined Lady, 'that can be remedied very easily and I am ready to move to any place you can indicate to me.' 'I am sorry,' said the Usher, 'but you must stay where you are till His Lordship cometh.' 'And what will happen,' said the Refined Lady, 'when His Lordship, as you are pleased to call Him, cometh?' 'That,' said the Usher, 'I am not able to tell you, but you will get the surprise of your life!'

The moral of this fable is easy to discern. It relates to the Last Judgment, which, according to Christian cosmology, decides the after-life of the 'dead souls'. Faithful to the letter and spirit of the Gospels, Claudel develops some of Jesus Christ's most scandalous and provocative utterances: the absurd concept that it is not sufficient to arrive at work on time to deserve better pay than the late-comers; the perverse idea that in 'My Father's Mansions' the poor have merits easier to reinvest than the treasures of the rich (do not the English talk of 'real-estate'?); the childish concept that Punch, the publican, always ends up by beating the Pharisee

policeman. The story the poet has chosen to illustrate these paradoxes stems from one of his most immortal dreams, one of his
most vivid visions, namely that the stage not only holds up the
human drama as a spectacle for mankind, but also reveals it to
the sight of the angels.

A high-society lady, one of those elegant, religious women
Claudel knew so well when he was a diplomatist, is getting ready
to cross the threshold of death. It is a critical moment that we are
about to live, as it were, in her company. It lasts no longer than a
vision, being timeless, yet it may be divided into three distinct
periods: (i) the choice, (ii) the metamorphosis, and (iii) the sudden
awakening.

The fine lady does not hesitate for a single moment between
the two passages in front of her in the foyer of the theatre. She
chooses the most comfortable, the one which slopes gently down
to the soft, downy seats in the stalls, lit by the friendly smile of
the ushers. The Upper Circle she sees in her dream resembles the
refined interiors of the sixteenth arrondissement rather than the
shabby-genteel dining-rooms of Malakoff or Vincennes.

As she steps into the hall, she is overcome by nausea. Is this
really a theatre? Surely the room looks more like a court-room.
Our refined lady notices a certain tautness and restlessness in all
the faces which surround her, some of which she recognizes. They
hardly acknowledge her greetings. Who are these ghastly people
who have been let into the hall and occupy the left half of it? And
where is her seat? And how confused the numbers are!

At last she hears an usher call out her name. Now she can calm
down again, she is going to be looked after, shown to her seat.
But the usher looks at her ticket, purses his lips and tells her that
she is on the wrong side. It had never occurred to her, right-
thinking soul that she is, that in this theatre everything is arranged
in relationship to the stage, right or left in relation to the Character
who is going to appear. She would like to correct her mistake, but
the usher objects. One is not allowed to change seats before His
Lordship arrives.

Such is the poem's line of development and what can be said

briefly about its subject matter and intent. One is immediately struck by the contrast between the economy of means and the powerful, suggestive effect. It is true that there are no colours in it, but everyone knows that parables, like dreams, are monochrome, constructed on a play of light and shade. There are no smells, no tactile sensations, for we have already passed into the beyond. However, the stifled, padded atmosphere of a luxury theatre besets us with such force that we can smell the furs, feel the velvet of the seats as we pass through a world of red and gold as unreal as wordly riches. Add to this the extremely skilful development of the narrative, which begins *ex abrupto*, and alternates direct narrative with indirect narrative, much as in a film. Thus the movement of the well-dressed people towards the stalls is conveyed to us through the contrast between the lady pausing before the two passages and the movement of the ushers coming to meet the play-goers. The checking of her ticket, whose colour is different from the others, tightens a strange dialectic spring, whose release contributes to the denouement of the poem. We are still in the room. But already an unexpected change is developing, with its transformation into a cold, sinister décor. This transformation is primarily mental: it corresponds to a deadening of the fine lady's sensitivity; she is no longer in tune with her environment; her superficial reflexes as a spectator and woman of the world work completely in a void. One notices in particular the 'psycho-syntactical' rejoinder: *How jolly and pleasant; But no! it was not pleasant and jolly at all*, on which the poem really hinges. At the same time the phrase *the more so* reminds us that the lady has continued to look in vain for her seat, an endeavour which is given gripping reality by the length of the passage dedicated to the analysis of her reactions. The story thus unfolds on two planes, the one being dependent on the other. Finally, the third part of the poem brings us back to direct narrative with the arrival of the usher and his dialogue with the fine lady, a passage in which Claudel's zest is given free rein.

But the image which can be deduced from the lineal development of a poem (Valéry doubted one could be deduced) barely reveals its surface meaning. Only a vertical cut through its fibre and structure is capable of disclosing the secret of its unity to us. *The Lady Who Always Did the Right Thing* owes its unity to a particular play on rhythms which produce an atmosphere, both unreal and concrete, whose growing tension finally resolves into humour.

These rhythms are all the more obvious because the text is written in a language over which Claudel did not have full mastery. Sometimes they are binary – *Theatre or Music Hall* . . . *fine and refined* . . . *Oily and smiling* . . . *one at my left, the other at my right* . . . – sustaining in our subconscious the alternatives that offered themselves to the refined lady from the first line, and prolonging the memory of the irrevocable choice which she has made. At other times they are ternary: *narrow, steep and rather dirty* . . . *all boisterous and mirthful and slightly intoxicated* . . . *stiff, silent, subtly hurt* (this last one is combined with the binary rhythm *decorously pained and congealed*) . . . *If I always take, If I insist, If I follow* . . . *by always doing, by always taking, by always following*. To an English ear these rhythms may sound rather strange. Indeed they are based on rhetorical habits which betray the Humanist education Claudel received at the Lycée Louis-le-Grand. They are combined in such a way as to suggest a clash between the lady's false mental stability and the instability of a situation of which she becomes aware only little by little.

Following a well-known Symbolist technique which one also finds in T. S. Eliot, the style of the piece presents us with an hybrid pattern. The sublime and the banal stand side by side with such ease, as to prove that the poet on no account wants to become his own dupe. Elegant sentences which reveal the hand of the essayist:

> The other passage, at the right hand, was a wide, spacious dignified porch, with thick carpets, tapestries, gracious statues and interesting pictures, gently sloping to the correct level . . .

are followed by slovenly ones:

> All well-dressed people, ladies and gentlemen, all people who

are counting for something, were going this way, amiably laughing, chattering and chafing each other, all ready to enjoy themselves to the utmost and to have a good time.

The Dantesque note in:

Thousands and thousands of men and women were there, all silent or talking quietly to each other.

is anti-climaxed by:

The Refined Lady looked through her face-à-main and was simply delighted . . .

Occasionally, the two dominant tones overlap in the same sentence:

The Refined Lady felt herself ill-at-ease and out-of-place in that grim judicial apartment, the more so as the numbers on her ticket were very confusing and she could not succeed in finding her seat.

This systematic de-mythification produces an odd effect unwittingly stressed by the solecisms through which transpire certain typically Claudelian turns of phrase: *the Hercules*, . . . *who are all counting* (a mis-use of the present continuous), *verified their tickets* (instead of *checked*), *who* (instead of *which*), *as strange* . . . (the *as* is superfluous), *all of her* . . . (the *of* is superfluous), *from a long time* . . . (*for* would be better), *suffering under* (*from* would be better), *they received* . . . (instead of *had received*), *so pleased* . . . (instead of *as pleased*), *I just looked* (instead of *I have been looking*), *Is it not here* (n'est ce pas là?), *as always told me my mother* (wrong word-order), *I can be no wrong* (do?), *at my right* (instead of *on*; this mistake is constant). . . . But these faults are perhaps less irritating than those T. S. Eliot, and to a lesser extent Ezra Pound, committed in the French poems they were rash enough to publish:

Mais une nuit d'été les voici à Ravenne,
A l'aise entre deux draps, chez deux centaines de punaises.[3]

Thanks to the subtle alteration of values performed by his solecisms, Claudel somehow enhances the impression of malaise and bewilderment we share with the exquisite lady. The general effect is all the more uncanny as the lapses do not exclude idiomatic phrases and touches which show a natural feeling for language: . . . *raw and vulgar gas-jets; have a good time; oily and smiling; introduced with a respectful bow; subdued appearance; simply delighted; gaily made inquiries; boisterous and mirthful and slightly intoxicated; grim, judicial apartment.*

The piece ends in a gem which emphasizes the syntactical parallelism of the two final sentences. *Cometh:* the archaism of the term confirms the various hints scattered throughout the text: 'Paradise' applied to the *Upper Circle*, the allusion to the *Midnight Court* ('Partage de minuit'?), the insistence on the term *Lordship*, with its legal and biblical associations. We understand only too well what the well-meaning people are waiting for.

By playing on the various shades of the word *right: go right; my right; do right; right nature; right side; declaration of rights* – that is the rights of men in general, and of the privileged in particular, with perhaps a dig at Protestant individualism and 'Action Française politics' – Claudel re-actualizes the heavenly protocol defined two thousand years ago by Jesus Christ, which reserves the best places for those who are in the worst positions. It is always *later* than one *thinks*.

We have delved deep enough to attempt an appraisal of *The Lady Who Always Did the Right Thing*. Let us state at once that, although the idea for this parable had been conceived long before it was written (the gas-jets!), it does not belong to Claudel's great period; it is to the myth of *Animus and Anima* what the *Livre de Christophe Colomb* is to the *Soulier de satin*. When the poet committed it to paper, the fruits had already fulfilled the promise of the flowers. And yet the interest of the piece is manifold. On the one hand, it offers an example of that poetic ambiguity so dear to Claudel, who uses it to emphasize the most challenging aspects of Christianity. Every word and sentence has a twofold content of humour and imagination. The total effect is perhaps rather heavy, but one must remember that the French poet's genius is made of flesh and blood, it has nothing of Shelley's disembodied idealism. Its wings propel both Ariel and Caliban through a medium thicker than ether. On the other hand, *The Lady Who Always Did the Right Thing* provides us with the elements of a diagnosis of Claudel's English and the manner in which he handled this tricky and glittering language which had always fascinated him. He knew it both too well and not well enough. In the parable of the lady, he muddles the verb tenses, especially the continual form; he shows uncertainty in the use of prepositions and in that of the article; yet, for all that, his English reads superbly. Through it we discern, insidiously refracted and distorted by a foreign idiom, some of the most typical inflexions of the great voice which is now silent.

NOTES

1. *America*, Sept. 1931. The text is reproduced in the appendix of *Œuvres Complètes*, *IX.*, Paris: Gallimard, 1961.
2. Cf. *Positions et Propositions*, I, Paris: Gallimard, 1925.
3. 'Lune de Miel', *Collected Poems*, New York: Harcourt, Brace & World, 1962, p. 28.

Select bibliography

PLAYS

Tête d'or (1st version), 1889, published 1890.
La Ville (1st version), 1890.
La Jeune Fille Violaine (1st version), 1892.
L'Échange (1st version), 1894.
Tête d'or (2nd version), 1894.
Le Repos du septième jour, 1896.
La Ville (2nd version), 1897.
La Jeune Fille Violaine (2nd version), 1898.
Partage de midi, 1905.
L'Annonce faite à Marie, 1910.
Protée (1st version), 1913.
Le Pain dur, 1914.
Le Père humilié, 1916.
Le Soulier de satin, 1924.
Le Livre de Christophe Colomb, 1927.
Jeanne d'Arc au bûcher, 1935.

These, and other plays, are available in the *Œuvres complètes* published in two volumes in the Bibliothèque de la Pléiade, 1956.

Claudel's verse is available in the *Œuvres poétique*, published in the Bibliothèque de la Pléiade, 1957.

A large selection of his prose, chosen and annotated by Jacques Petit and Charles Galpérine, was published in the Bibliothèque de la Pléiade in 1965, under the title *Œuvres en prose*.